GOOD ADVICE

GOOD ADVICE

COMPILED BY

WILLIAM SAFIRE & LEONARD SAFIR

ILLUSTRATIONS BY

MONICA SHEEHAN

WINGS BOOKS · NEW YORK

This 1992 edition is published by Wings Books,
a division of Random House Value Publishing, Inc.,
201 East 50th Street, New York, New York 10022,
by arrangement with Times Books.

Wings Books and colophon are trademarks of Random House Value Publishing, Inc.

Random House
New York • Toronto • London • Sydney • Auckland
http://www.randomhouse.com/

Printed and bound in the United States of America

Library of Congress Cataloging-in-Publication Data

Good advice / compiled by Leonard Safir and William Safire.
     p.   cm.
  Originally published: New York : Times Books, 1982.
  Includes index.
  ISBN 0-517-08473-2
  1. Quotations, English.   2. Conduct of life—Quotations, maxims,
etc. I. Safir, Leonard.   II. Safire, William, 1929–
[PN6081.G63   1992]
082—dc20   92-18842
                                                              CIP

18   17   16   15   14   13   12

To our Mother and Father

Ida Panish Safir

and

Oliver Crouse Safir

"It is the duty, and ought to be the pleasure, of age and experience to warn and instruct youth and to come to the aid of experience. When sailors have discovered rocks or breakers, and have had the good luck to escape with life from amidst them, they, unless they be pirates or barbarians as well as sailors, point out the spots for the placing of buoys and of lights, in order that others may not be exposed to the danger which they have so narrowly escaped. What man of common humanity, having, by good luck, missed being engulfed in a quagmire or quicksand, will withhold from his neighbors a knowledge of the peril without which the dangerous spots are not to be approached?"

—WILLIAM COBBETT,
"Advice To Young Men And
(incidentally) To Young Women
In The Middle and Higher
Ranks Of Life." 1829

CONTENTS

ON GOOD ADVICE

HERE'S SOME GOOD ADVICE: GET GOOD ADVICE.

Easier said than done. Where do you get it, and what does it cost? More to the point, how can you be sure that what is "good" advice for others may not be the worst kind of advice for you? And once you get the advice, are you obligated to take it? If you reject it, have you lost an adviser and gained an I-told-you-so?

People in need of advice, which they often derogate as "a few good steers," do not torture themselves with such questions. If you need it, you know it, and more often than not you are willing to use at least part of the guidance you get from people you trust.

As a result, the advice business is booming. Fortune-tellers now bill themselves as "readers and advisers"; press agents have stopped calling themselves public relations counsels and have adopted "public affairs adviser"; Presidential aides who used to hang around the Oval Office and toss in a few ideas are now institutionalized as National Security Advisor and Chairman of the Council of Economic Advisers. Even Lexicographers are arguing about the spelling of the vogue word: does the old "adviser" remain preferred, or has the frequent misspelling of "advisor," on the analogy of "supervisor," made the variant form correct? (My advice: stick to "adviser.")

In this era of how-to, with books of specialized advice on ways to improve your backswing or surefire methods to lose weight without sniveling, it occurred to my brother, Len, that no book exists that brings together the best advice on good ways to live the good life.

Where is guidance from wise—or, at least, experienced—guides, arranged in categories that enable the advisee to get a quick philosophical fix? Quotation books abound, wise sayings proliferate, and aphorisms are endlessly anthologized, but where is the line that actually directs you to act—that tells you what to do? You can find dozens of paeans to "commitment" and "dedication," which are fine and instructive, but where is the imperative needle that gets you off your duff?

My favorite in this collection of directions for living is Napoleon's "If you start to take Vienna—take Vienna." There's a verb in that quotation that shows the way. Not a lot of talk about the need to follow through on a commitment, or about the dangers of appearing indecisive, but a pristine point—"take Vienna." Once you have tossed your hat over the wall, climb the wall; don't turn back. That's good advice.

The essence of advice is a verb—do this or do that, or never do either. "He who hesitates is lost" is a nice observation, but "Look before you leap" is advice. Some of the guidance herein lacks the terseness that can be chiseled over a small doorway—for example, Polonius' famous advice to Laertes rambles over many subjects, but finally comes to a point with "To thine own self be true, And it must follow, as the night the day, Thou canst not then be false to any man." But the cleverest advice, the common denominator, is a clear direction. "Never complain and never explain." (So why do we need an introduction?) That's not an example of good advice. Disraeli is the one most often credited with "never complain and never explain," and his motto was taken up by Henry Ford II, but it advises arrogant stoicism. Because I liked its directness and banged my spoon against the highchair, my brother Len included it, but under a catchall "Bad Advice," along with the line misattributed to W. C. Fields, "Never give a sucker an even break." Quotable line, useful for wise-guys, but hardly good advice. Disraeli's counsel on partisanship, "Damn principle! Stick to your party," is included under "Questionable Advice"—not good, but perhaps not always bad.

Clever quips by celebrities were eschewed and spat out. "The way to fight a woman," advised John Barrymore, "is with your hat—grab it and run." Worth a smile, but it's not serious advice. Nor is the famous quotation from Albert Einstein: "If A equals success, then the formula is A equals X plus Y plus Z. X is work. Y is play. Z is keep your mouth shut." He was being quotably outrageous, but not being helpful.

A word about historical accuracy: many sayings attributed to famous people were never said by them, as Marie "Let them eat cake" Antoinette would be the first to agree. The "editing of history" is helped along by a speechwriter who takes a long, pompous sentence by Grover Cleveland and sharpens it into "public office is a public trust." Some of the advice herein comes from secondary sources, and has probably been rubbed smooth; read it more for the advice than for the scholarly certainty about original phrasing.

For example, a colorful piece of folk advice is that attributed to Satchel Paige, the black baseball pitcher, listed under "Health," which begins "Avoid fried meats which angry up the blood" and concludes "Don't look back. Something might be gaining on you." The amusing and useful passage was concocted by Richard Donovan, a writer for *Collier's* magazine, in a 1953 profile on the ageless athlete: the writer was asked by the editor for "typical Paige quotes" to use in a box, breaking up a column of type. He cooked up the famous counsel, which Paige happily accepted as his own after it appeared. It is listed herein as "attributed to Satchel Paige."

In the same way, I interviewed adman Bruce Barton in the early fifties and took down a couple of boring sentences on the importance of change. In writing the interview (I was young and irresponsible), I quoted him briskly with "Keep changing. When you're through changing, you're through." *Reader's Digest* reprinted the aphorism, and Barton used it in all subsequent speeches—I presume he thought it was original. In writing a presidential address for Richard Nixon, I re-used it—"As Bruce Barton once said, 'when you're through changing, you're through.'" And here it is being used again. I'm not changing it, and I'm not through. (If I had to re-cast that quote as advice, it would read: "Never say you're through changing unless you're prepared to admit you're through.")

Which brings us to the artificial production of aphorisms. Some writers—Oscar Wilde, Elbert Hubbard—prided themselves on producing a gem-like line that reeked with wisdom. Other writers produced aphorisms in the course of a play or piece—William Shakespeare or Bernard Shaw, to name a couple. The natural aphorism, springing out of a situation or a line of thought, is usually better advice than the prettily balanced line created to be quoted.

The reader may be wondering who this Aphor was, anyway, to be the patron saint of the pithily wise. That's folk etymology—there was no Aphor. The word "aphorism" is rooted in the Greek aphorizein, a division or section of the horizon, which is an apt figure for a little piece of truth. No advice reveals the whole truth; but start with a slice that is true for you, and work outward.

This digression into etymology reveals another reason for this book: As a self-certified language maven, usage dictator, and pop grammarian, I have seen with my own eyes the fierceness of the demand for moorings. People want to know what "presently" means—"now," or "in a little while"? (Advice: Forget the word, it has lost its meaning. Use "now" or "soon," depending on which you mean. I'll explain why momentarily.) People also want to know whether "parameters" is a vogue word or a useful new term. (Advice: In mathematics, it means a "variable constant," but in general usage, it has come to mean "characteristics or dimensions"; use it to help define a problem or situation.) Going beyond detail to principle, should "Black English" be accepted in schools in black neighborhoods? (No: A dialect is for the home and the in-group, not for communication with the outside world.)

The hunger for advice in the language field reflects the general appetite for direction. Lead us, we say to our leaders, and we'll love you—but just don't get too far out in front of the parade. Boldness (usually followed by compromise) is a virtue; timidity (usually followed by a belatedly bold lashing-out) is a vice. Tell us what you're trying to do; tell us what you want of us; if it is within reason, we'll give it a try, and if it does not work, we will turn to other leaders with other advice.

Is this grasping for guidance a good sign? I think so; we can use a little followership to give our leaders confidence. The trouble begins when we become mesmerized by advice, when we are transfixed by expertise, when we look lemming-like for direction to faith healers, backswing experts, diet-creators, business intimidators, and pseudo-analysts, following them and their how-to bromides out to sea.

The best advice is the kind that you choose with care and then shape to fit your matter and your moment. (Thank you, Aphor.) Here is a compilation of serious guidance from helpful people across the ages: "Ask counsel of both times," suggested Francis Bacon, "of the ancient time what is best; and of the latter time what is fittest." When the advice conflicts, or points in somewhat divergent directions, it is up to you to choose what best fits your circumstance and your character.

"Whatever advice you give," advised Horace, "be short." Okay. Start anywhere, or start with a current anxiety, but as Napoleon would say—if you start to take Vienna, take Vienna.

—WILLIAM SAFIRE

ACHIEVEMENT · ACTION · ADOLESCENCE/YOUTH · ADVERTISING · AIM · AMBITION · ANGER

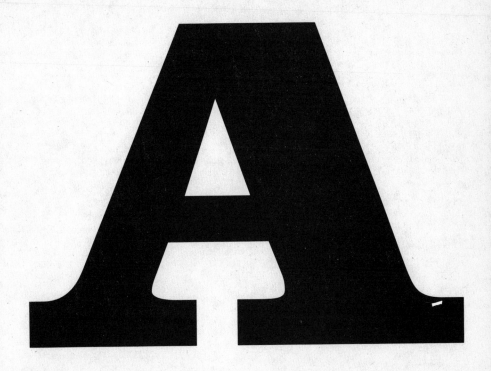

APPEARANCE · ARGUMENT · ART · ASKING/SEEKING · ASPIRATION · ASSERTIVENESS · ATTITUDE

Achievement

WHATEVER THY HAND findeth to do, do it with all thy might. —Old Testament

HAVING ONCE DECIDED to achieve a certain task, achieve it at all costs of tedium and distaste. The gain in self-confidence of having accomplished a tiresome labor is immense.

—Arnold Bennett

SUCCESS IS NOT so much achievement as achieving. Refuse to join the cautious crowd that plays not to lose; play to win.

—David J. Mahoney

YOU MAY BE disappointed if you fail, but you are doomed if you don't try.

—Beverly Sills

Let us then be up and doing
With a heart for any fate
Still achieving, still pursuing
Learn to labor and to wait.

—Henry Wadsworth Longfellow

MY MOTHER DREW a distinction between achievement and success. She said that "achievement is the knowledge that you have studied and worked hard and done the best that is in you. Success is being praised by others, and that's nice, too, but not as important or satisfying. Always aim for achievement and forget about success."

—Helen Hayes

Action

BEGIN AT ONCE to live . . .

—Seneca

If you really want to live you'd better start at once to try.
If you don't it really doesn't matter, but you'd better start to die.

—W. H. Auden

GET ACTION. DO things; be sane, don't fritter away your time . . . take a place wherever you are and be somebody; get action.　　—Theodore Roosevelt

TRUST ONLY MOVEMENT. Life happens at the level of events not of words. Trust movement.

—Alfred Adler

ACT QUICKLY, THINK slowly.

—Greek proverb

WE ARE MADE for action, and for right action—for thought and for true thought. Let us live while we live; let us be alive and doing; let us act on what we have, since we have not what we wish.　　—John Henry Cardinal Newman

MAKE UP YOUR mind to act decidedly and take the consequences. No good is ever done in this world by hesitation. —Thomas Henry Huxley

WE MUST LEARN to be still in the midst of activity and to be vibrantly alive in repose. —Indira Gandhi

Adolescence/Youth

IF YOU REFUSE to be made straight when you are green, you will not be made straight when you are dry. —African proverb

TODAY . . . YOU ARE prodded to "project an image" to the world. One way of projecting an attractive image is to carry the human body with style—to stand, sit and move with verve, pride, elasticity and grace. —Enid A. Haupt

BESTOW THY YOUTH so that thou mayest have comfort to remember it when it hath forsaken thee, and not sigh and grieve at the account thereof. While thou art young thou wilt think it will never have an end; but the longest day hath its evening, and thou shalt enjoy it but once; it never turns again; use it therefore as the spring-time, which soon departeth, and wherein thou oughtest to plant and sow all provisions for a long and happy life. —Sir Walter Raleigh

WHAT CAN I say to you? I am perhaps the oldest musician in the world. I am an old man, but in many senses a very young man. And this is what I want you to be, young, young all your life, and to say things to the world that are true.
—Pablo Casals

DON'T BITE THE hand that has your allowance in it.
—Paul Dickson
(quoting Lois Tidler, a youngster)

Advertising

THE MORE FACTS you tell, the more you sell. An advertisement's chance for success invariably increases as the number of pertinent merchandise facts included in the advertisement increases.
—Dr. Charles Edwards

BUY CHEAP, SELL DEAR.
—Thomas Lodge, 1595

NEVER WRITE AN advertisement which you wouldn't want your own family to read. You wouldn't tell lies to your own wife. Don't tell them to mine. Do as you would be done by. If you tell lies about a product, you will be found out—either by the Government, which will prosecute you, or by the consumer, who will punish you by not buying your product a second time. Good products can be sold by *honest* advertising. If you don't think the product is good, you have no business to be advertising it.
—David M. Ogilvy

BIG IDEAS ARE so hard to recognize, so fragile, so easy to kill. Don't forget that, all of you who don't have them.
—John Elliott, Jr.

(*See also* Business, Labor, Management, and Work Psychology.)

Aim

FIRST SAY TO yourself what you would be; and then do what you have to do.
—Epictetus

HITCH YOUR WAGON to a star. Let us not fag in paltry works which serve our pot and bag alone. Let us not lie or steal. No god will help. We shall find all their teams going the other way; every god will leave us. Work rather for those inter-

ests which the divinities honor and promote—justice, love, freedom, knowledge, utility. —Ralph Waldo Emerson

MAKE NO LITTLE plans; they have no magic to stir men's blood. . . . Make
big plans, aim high in hope and work. —Daniel H. Burnham

AIM AT THE sun, and you may not reach it; but your arrow will fly higher than
if aimed at an object on a level with yourself. —Joel Hawes

IT IS NOT enough to aim; you must hit. —Italian proverb

SLIGHT NOT WHAT'S near, while aiming at what's far. —Euripides, *Rhesus*

Ambition

KEEP AWAY FROM people who try to belittle your ambitions. Small people
always do that, but the really great make you feel that you, too, can become
great. —Mark Twain

> Stick to your sphere;
> Or, if you insist, as you have the right,
> On spreading your wings for a loftier flight,
> The moral is,—Take care where you light.
>
> —J. T. Trowbridge

HE WHO WOULD leap high must take a long run. —Danish proverb

FIRST, YOU MUST be ambitious, but you must not be so nakedly aggressive
that your fellow workers rise up and destroy you. *Tout soldat porte dans sa*

giberne le bâton de maréchal. [Every soldier has a marshal's baton in his knapsack.] Yes, but don't let it stick out.
—David M. Ogilvy

> Be wise;
> Soar not too high to fall; but stoop to rise.
>
> —Philip Massinger

CHILDREN, YOU MUST remember something. A man without ambition is dead. A man with ambition but no love is dead. A man with ambition and love for his blessings here on earth is ever so alive. Having been alive, it won't be so hard in the end to lie down and rest.
—Pearl Bailey

YOU GOTTA GET a gimmick if you wanta get ahead.—Veteran stripper in *Gypsy*

Anger

IF YOU WOULD cure anger, do not feed it. Say to yourself: "I used to be angry every day; then every other day; now only every third or fourth day." When you reach thirty days offer a sacrifice of thanksgiving to the gods.
—Epictetus

NEVER FORGET WHAT a man says to you when he is angry.—Henry Ward Beecher

WHEN ANGER RISES, think of the consequences.
—Confucius

THE GREAT THING, when you are angry, is to kick, if only in fantasy, anybody or anything but yourself.
—Brendan Francis

WHEN ANGRY, COUNT four; when very angry, swear.
—Mark Twain

NEVER DO ANYTHING when you are in a temper, for you will do everything wrong.
—Baltasar Gracian

ANGER IS WHAT arouses you to challenge a situation. Aim to use it to improve things. Often, with it, you can change things. —Walter McQuade and Anna Aikman

EAT A THIRD and drink a third and leave the remaining third of your stomach empty. Then, when you get angry, there will be sufficient room for your rage.
—Babylonian Talmud, tractate Gittin

ROUSE NOT THE anger of a multitude, though it be but a nest of wasps.
—John Lancaster Spalding

DON'T BE AFRAID to express anger (hiding it is even more stressful than letting it out), but choose your fights; don't hassle over every little thing. . . . You can also give in once in a while, instead of always insisting you are right and others are wrong.
—Jane E. Brody

NEVER WRITE A letter while you are angry.
—Chinese proverb

Appearance

KEEP UP APPEARANCES whatever you do.
—Charles Dickens

YOUR FIRST APPEARANCE, he said to me, is the gauge by which you will be measured; try to manage that you may go beyond yourself in after times, but beware of ever doing less.
—Jean Jacques Rousseau

DON'T WORRY ABOUT your physical shortcomings (I am no Greek god). Don't get too much sleep and don't tell anybody your troubles. Appearances count:

Get a sun lamp to keep you looking as though you have just come back from somewhere expensive; maintain an elegant address even if you have to live in the attic. . . . Never niggle when short of cash. Borrow big, but always repay promptly.
— Aristotle Onassis

THE BEST WAY to attract money, she had discovered, was to give the appearance of having it.
— Gail Sheehy

BEWARE SO LONG as you live, of judging people by appearances.
— La Fontaine

IF I LOOK fabulous or if I look haggard and awful, it's the lighting. . . . When I appear on a program which is well-lit I look five years younger. So you can imagine that my first advice to women concerned about their appearance is to check the lights in their living room.
— Barbara Walters

SUNBURN IS VERY becoming—but only when it is even—one must be careful not to look like a mixed grill.
— Noel Coward

WE ARE CHARMED by neatness of person; let not thy hair be out of order.—Ovid

KEEPING YOUR CLOTHES well pressed will keep you from looking hard pressed.
— Coleman Cox

DO NOT JUDGE men by mere appearances; for the light laughter that bubbles on the lip often mantles over the depths of sadness, and the serious look may be the sober veil that covers a divine peace and joy.
— E. H. Chapin

Argument

THE BEST WAY I know to win an argument is to start by being in the right.

—Lord Hailsham

NEVER ARGUE; REPEAT your assertion.

—Robert Owen

> I beg you, do not be unchangeable.
> Do not believe that you alone can be right.
> The man who thinks that,
> The man who maintains that only he has the power
> To reason correctly, the gift to speak, the soul—
> A man like that, when you know him, turns out empty.

—Sophocles

IF YOU WOULD convince others, seem open to conviction yourself.

—Philip Dormer Stanhope (Lord Chesterfield)

IF YOU GO in for argument, take care of your temper. Your logic, if you have any, will take care of itself.

—Joseph Farrell

BEFORE YOU CONTRADICT an old man, my fair friend, you should endeavor to understand him.

—George Santayana

IF YOU CAN'T answer a man's argument, all is not lost; you can still call him vile names.

—Elbert Hubbard

AUDI PARTEM ALTERUM. (Hear the other side.)

—Saint Augustine

Art

WE SHOULD COMPORT ourselves with the masterpieces of art as with exalted personages—stand quietly before them and wait till they speak to us.

—Arthur Schopenhauer

WE HAVE AN interval and then our place knows us no more. . . . Our one chance lies in expanding that interval, in getting as many pulsations as possible into the given time. Great passions may give us this quickened sense of life, ecstasy and sorrow of love, the various forms of enthusiastic activity, disinterested or otherwise, which come naturally to many of us. Only be sure it is passion—that it does yield you this fruit of a quickened, multiplied consciousness. Of such wisdom, the poetic passion, the desire of beauty, the love of art for its own sake, has most. For art comes to you proposing frankly to give nothing but the highest quality to your moments as they pass, and simply for those moments' sake.

—Walter Pater

EVERY YOUNG ARTIST has to do it one way, his way, and the hell with patterns. Remember who you are and where you are and what you're doing. Nobody else can do anything for you and you really wouldn't want them to, anyway. And never take advice, including this.

—Katherine Anne Porter

ART SHOULD BE appreciated with passion and violence, not with a tepid, depreciating elegance that fears the censoriousness of a common room.

—W. Somerset Maugham

(*See also* Painting.)

Asking/Seeking

Ask, and it shall be given you;
Seek, and ye shall find;
Knock, and it shall be opened unto you:
For every one that asketh receiveth;
And he that seeketh findeth;
And to him that knocketh it shall be opened.

—Jesus of Nazareth

WHAT WE SEEK we shall find; what we flee from flees from us; . . . and hence the high caution, that, since we are sure of having what we wish, we beware to ask only for high things. —Ralph Waldo Emerson

GO, SEEKER, IF you will, throughout the land. . . . Observe the whole of it, survey it as you might survey a field. . . . It's your oyster—yours to open if you will. . . . Just make yourself at home, refresh yourself, get the feel of things, adjust your sights, and get the scale. . . . To every man his chance—to every man, regardless of his birth, his shining, golden opportunity—to every man the right to live, to work, to be himself, and to become whatever thing his manhood and his vision can combine to make him—this, seeker, is the promise of America. —Thomas Wolfe

KNOW HOW TO ask. There is nothing more difficult for some people, nor for others, easier. —Baltasar Gracian

ASK A LOT, but take what is offered. —Russian proverb

Aspiration

Climb High
Climb Far
Your goal the sky
Your aim the star.

—Inscription on Hopkins Memorial Steps
Williams College
Williamstown, Massachusetts

IF YOU ASPIRE to the highest place, it is no disgrace to stop at the second, or even the third, place.

—Cicero

LOOK TO A gown of gold, and you will at least get a sleeve of it.

—Sir Walter Scott

Ah, but a man's reach should exceed his grasp
Or what's a heaven for?

—Robert Browning

Assertiveness

YOU WILL NOT be discouraged if the world does not rush to you, demanding what you have. . . . Neither will you quietly sit down to let the world wonder and then seek you; but you will be aggressive; you will carry your truths to people and cause them to see them so clearly that they must accept them.

—Edith Kincaid Butler

TO KNOW ONESELF, one should assert oneself. —Albert Camus

I WOULD LIKE to amend the idea of being in the right place at the right time. There are many people who were in the right place at the right time but didn't know it. You have to recognize when the right place and the right time fuse and take advantage of that opportunity. There are plenty of opportunities out there. You can't sit back and wait. —Ellen Metcalf

VIGOROUS LET US be in attaining our ends, and mild in our method of attainment. —Motto of Lord Newborough

IF YOU ASPIRE to anything better than politics, expect no cooperation from men. They will not further anything good. You must prevail of your own force, as a plant springs and grows by its own vitality. —Henry David Thoreau

Bite off more than you can chew,
  Then chew it.
Plan more than you can do,
  Then do it.

—Anonymous

Attitude

IF YOUR DAILY life seems poor, do not blame it; blame yourself, tell yourself that you are not poet enough to call forth its riches. —Rainer Maria Rilke

HOWEVER MEAN YOUR life is, meet it and live it; do not shun and call it hard names. It is not so bad as you are. It looks poorest when you are richest. The fault-finder will find faults even in Paradise. Love your life.—Henry David Thoreau

ALWAYS FALL IN with what you're asked to accept. Take what is given, and make it over your way. My aim in life has always been to hold my own with whatever's going. Not against: with.

—Robert Frost

WHEN FATE HANDS us a lemon, let's try to make a lemonade. —Dale Carnegie

BAD ADVICE · BEAUTY · BEGINNINGS · BETTERMENT · BOLDNESS · BOOKS

BOREDOM/EXCITEMENT · BROTHERHOOD · BUILDING/ARCHITECTURE · BUSINESS

Bad Advice

AND REMEMBER, DEARIE, never give a sucker an even break.

—Attributed to W. C. Fields,
though the line is from Act II of
Dorothy Donnelly's *Poppy*

DECIDE PROMPTLY, BUT never give your reasons. Your decisions may be right, but your reasons are sure to be wrong. —Lord Mansfield

NEVER COMPLAIN AND never explain. —Benjamin Disraeli,
quote adopted by Henry Ford II

FIRST SECURE AN independent income, then practice virtue. —Greek proverb

ANSWER VIOLENCE WITH VIOLENCE! —Juan Perón

BE ON THY guard against the good and the just! They would fain crucify those who devise their own virtue—they hate the lonesome ones.—Friedrich Nietzsche

Get place and wealth, if possible with grace;
If not, by any means get wealth and place.

—Alexander Pope

CALUMNIATE! CALUMNIATE! SOME of it will always stick.

—Pierre Augustin Caron de Beaumarchais

HAVE NO FRIENDS equal to yourself. —Confucius

HERE'S THE RULE for bargains: "Do other men, for they would do you." That's the true business precept.   —Jonas Chuzzlewit, in Charles Dickens' *Martin Chuzzlewit*

(WHEN TOLD THE people had no bread): Let them eat cake.
                                                      —Attributed (falsely) to Marie Antoinette

> Damn with faint praise, assent with civil leer,
> And, without sneering, teach the rest to sneer.
>
> —Alexander Pope

I THINK PEOPLE still want to marry rich. Girls especially. . . . [It's] simple. Don't date poor boys. Go where the rich are. . . . You don't have to be rich to go where they go.   —Sheilah Graham

THE SECRET OF life is never to have an emotion that is unbecoming.
                                                      —Oscar Wilde

WIN ANY WAY you can as long as you can get away with it. Nice guys finish last.   —Leo Durocher

IF AN INJURY has to be done to a man it should be so severe that his vengeance need not be feared.

I JUDGE IMPETUOSITY to be better than caution; for Fortune is a woman, and if you wish to master her, you must strike and beat her.   —Niccolò Machiavelli

HAVING MENTIONED LAUGHING, I must particularly warn you against it; and I could heartily wish that you may often be seen to smile, but never heard to laugh, while you live . . . In my mind there is nothing so illiberal and so ill-bred as audible laughter.   —Lord Chesterfield

REGARD THE SOCIETY of women as a necessary unpleasantness of social life, and avoid it as much as possible. —Leo Tolstoy, from his diary

BE COMMONPLACE AND creeping, and you will be a success.
—Pierre Augustin Caron de Beaumarchais

SUFFER WOMEN ONCE to arrive at an equality with you, and they will from that moment become your superiors. —Cato the Elder

IN THE FIGHT between you and the world, back the world. —Franz Kafka

EXERCISE IS BUNK. If you are healthy, you don't need it; if you are sick, you shouldn't take it. —Henry Ford

(*See also* Counsel, Facetious Advice, Questionable Advice, and Fatherly Advice.)

Beauty

I DON'T THINK of all the misery, but of the beauty that still remains. . . . My advice is: Go outside, to the fields, enjoy nature and the sunshine, go out and try to recapture happiness in yourself and in God. Think of all the beauty that's still left in and around you and be happy! —Anne Frank

TAKE NOTHING FOR granted as beautiful or ugly, but take every building to pieces, and challenge every feature. Learn to distinguish the curious from the beautiful. Get the habit of analysis—analysis will in time enable synthesis to become your habit of mind. "Think in simples" as my old master used to say—meaning to reduce the whole of its parts in simplest terms, getting back to first principles. —Frank Lloyd Wright

NEVER LOSE AN opportunity of seeing anything that is beautiful; for beauty is God's handwriting—a wayside sacrament. Welcome it in every fair face, in every fair sky, in every fair flower, and thank God for it as a cup of blessing.

—Ralph Waldo Emerson

BEAUTY IS A thing severe and unapproachable, never to be won by a languid lover. You must lie in wait for her coming and take her unawares, press her hard and clasp her in a tight embrace, and force her to yield. —Honoré de Balzac

WHEN YOU HAVE only two pennies left in the world, buy a loaf of bread with one, and a lily with the other. —Chinese proverb

Beginnings

BEGIN; TO BEGIN is half the work. Let half still remain; again begin this, and thou wilt have finished. —Ausonius

DARE TO BE wise; begin! He who postpones the hour of living rightly is like the rustic who waits for the river to run out before he crosses. —Horace

SET OUT WISELY at first; custom will make every virtue more easy and pleasant to you than any vice can be. —English proverb

BEFORE YOU BEGIN a thing, remind yourself that difficulties and delays quite impossible to foresee are ahead. If you could see them clearly, naturally you could do a great deal to get rid of them but you can't. You can only see one thing clearly and that is your goal. Form a mental vision of that and cling to it through thick and thin. —Kathleen Norris

LET US WATCH well our beginnings, and results will manage themselves. —Alexander Clark

If well thou hast begun, go on foreright;
It is the end that crowns us, not the fight.

—Robert Herrick

Betterment

SLUMBER NOT IN the tents of your fathers. The world is advancing. Advance with it.

—Giuseppe Mazzini

IT IS NECESSARY to try to surpass oneself always; this occupation ought to last as long as life.

—Christina, Queen of Sweden, 1629–89

WE MUST ALWAYS change, renew, rejuvenate ourselves; otherwise we harden.

—Goethe

Build thee more stately mansions,
O my soul,
As the swift seasons roll!
Leave thy low-vaulted past!

Let each new temple, nobler than the last,
Shut thee from heaven with a dome more vast,
Till thou at length are free,
Leaving thine outgrown shell by
    life's unresting sea!

—Oliver Wendell Holmes

YOU'VE GOT TO do your own growing, no matter how tall your grandfather was.

—Irish proverb

Boldness

"Be bold! be bold!" and everywhere—"Be bold;
Be not too bold!" Yet better the excess
Than the defect; better the more than less.

—Henry Wadsworth Longfellow

YOU'VE GOT TO be brave and you've got to be bold. Brave enough to take your chance on your own discriminations—what's right and what's wrong, what's good and what's bad.

—Robert Frost

What you can do, or dream
you can, begin it;
Boldness has genius, power
and magic in it.

—Goethe

BE BOLD AND mighty powers will come to your aid.

—Basil King

Books

LEARN TO LOVE good books. There are treasures in books that all the money of the world cannot buy, but that the poorest laborer can have for nothing.

—Robert G. Ingersoll

SPEAK OF THE moderns without contempt and of the ancients without idolatry; judge them by their merits, but not by their age. —Lord Chesterfield

IF YOU CANNOT read all your books, at any rate handle them, and, as it were, fondle them. Let them fall open where they will. . . . Make a voyage of discovery, taking soundings of uncharted seas.

—Sir Winston Churchill

PICK YOUR BOOKS as you would your friends. Have Emerson in your home. Ever see a movie that was a bit over your head? Well—it was because you haven't read enough.

—Fiorello H. La Guardia

NEVER READ A book through merely because you have begun it.

—John Witherspoon

BEWARE OF A man of one book.

—English proverb

MASTER BOOKS, BUT do not let them master you. Read to live, not live to read.

—Edward George Bulwer-Lytton

BE AS CAREFUL of the books you read, as of the company you keep; for your habits and character will be as much influenced by the former as by the latter.

—Paxton Hood

THE BOOK TO read is not the one which thinks for you, but the one which makes you think.

—James McCosh

EVERY LITTLE WHILE another man decides what are the best books. Pay not attention to him, and decide yourself.

—E. W. Howe

WEAR THE OLD coat and buy the new book.

—Austin Phelps

Boredom/Excitement

SAVE THE FLEETING minute; learn gracefully to dodge the bore.

—Sir William Osler

WHEN A THING bores you, do not do it. Do not pursue a fruitless perfection.

—Ferdinand Victor Eugene Delacroix

THE SECRET OF making one's self tiresome is not to know when to stop.

—Voltaire

THINK EXCITEMENT, TALK excitement, act out excitement, and you are bound to become an excited person. Life will take on a new zest, deeper interest and greater meaning. You can think, talk and act yourself into dullness or into monotony or into unhappiness. By the same process you can build up inspiration, excitement and a surging depth of joy. —Norman Vincent Peale

WHAT IS REQUIRED is sight and insight—then you might add one more: excite.

—Robert Frost

Brotherhood

HELP THY BROTHER'S boat across, and lo! thine own has reached the shore.

—Hindu proverb

TO LIVE IS not to live for oneself alone; let us help one another. —Menander

NO MAN IS an Island, entire of it selfe; every man is a peece of the Continent, a part of the maine; if a Clod bee washed away by the Sea, Europe is the lesse, as well as if a Promontorie were, as well as if a Manor of thy friends or of thine owne were; any man's death diminishes me, because I am involved in Mankinde; and therefore never send to know for whom the bell tolls: It tolls for thee. —John Donne

THERE'S HARDLY A place in the world where you don't know within an hour any event that's happened there. We *have* to live with one another.

—Michael J. Mansfield

Building/Architecture

WHEN WE BUILD, let us think that we build for ever. —John Ruskin

REGARD IT AS just as desirable to build a chicken house as to build a cathedral. The size of the project means little in art, beyond the money matter. It is the quality of character that really counts. Character may be large in the little or little in the large. —Frank Lloyd Wright

ALWAYS DESIGN A thing by considering it in its next larger context—a chair in a room, a room in a house, a house in an environment, an environment in a city plan. —Eliel Saarinen

LESS IS MORE.
God is in the details. —Mies van der Rohe

ONCE YOU SINK that first stake, they'll never make you pull it up.—Robert Moses

Business

DON'T OPEN A shop unless you know how to smile. —Jewish proverb

LIVE TOGETHER LIKE brothers and do business like strangers. —Arab proverb

NEVER FEAR THE want of business. A man who qualifies himself well for his calling, never fails of employment. —Thomas Jefferson

THE SECRET OF business is to know something that nobody else knows. —Aristotle Onassis

THINK OF EASE, but work on. —English proverb

> Try novelties for salesman's bait,
> For novelty wins everyone.

EVERYTHING WHICH IS properly *business* we must keep carefully separate from life. Business requires earnestness and method; life must have a freer handling. —Goethe

BEAT YOUR GONG and sell your candies. —Chinese proverb

BUSINESS ENGLISH: WRITE as if you believe your correspondent to be intelligent; write as compactly, briefly, simply and directly as you can; keep closely to the point; write as if you are not only responsible for what you write but also responsible for what you do; be polite and pleasant.

ALWAYS DEFINE YOUR TERMS. —Eric Partridge

IF YOU THINK about it, you can probably recall hundreds of incidents where you ended up poorer because you failed to speak up, because you were afraid to ask for more information—"How much does it actually cost?"—because you were afraid to suggest a possible solution for fear of seeming pushy. At the time of making a purchase, for instance, there is usually room to better your position. Overcome shyness, and help yourself make it in your world! Ask the dealer, "How much is your realistic bottom price?" After you hear it, you already have saved a good bit in case you buy.

—Roy M. Cohn

FIRST THINK OF bread, and then of the bride.

—Norwegian proverb

(*See also* Advertising, Labor, Management, and Work Psychology.)

CALMNESS/COOLNESS · CANDOR · CAPABILITY · CAREER · CAUTION

C

CHANGE · CHARACTER · CHARITY · CHEERFULNESS · CHILDREN

Calmness/Coolness

BE CALM IN arguing; for fierceness makes error a fault, and truth discourtesy; calmness is a great advantage. —George Herbert

KEEP COOL; ANGER is not an argument. —Daniel Webster

REPROVE NOT, IN their wrath, excited men; good counsel comes all out of season then; but when their fury is appeased and past, they will perceive their faults, and mend at last. When he is cool and calm, then utter it.—John Randolph

KEEP COOL AND you command everybody. —Louis de Saint-Just

ALWAYS BEHAVE LIKE a duck—keep calm and unruffled on the surface but paddle like the devil underneath. —Jacob Braude

DON'T THINK THERE are no crocodiles because the water is calm.
—Malayan proverb

Candor

SAY WHAT YOU have to say, not what you ought. Any truth is better than make-believe. —Henry David Thoreau

ALWAYS BE READY to speak your mind and a base man will avoid you.
—William Blake

IF INDEED YOU must be candid, be candid beautifully. —Kahlil Gibran

BE YOURSELF AND speak your mind today, though it contradict all you have said before.
—Elbert Hubbard

Capability

WHENEVER YOU ARE asked if you can do a job, tell 'em, "Certainly I can!" Then get busy and find out how to do it.
—Theodore Roosevelt

NOW IN ORDER that people may be happy in their work these three things are needed:

They must be fit for it;
They must not do too much of it.
And they must have a sense of success in it—not a doubtful sense, such as needs some testimony of other people for its confirmation, but a sure sense, or rather knowledge, that so much work has been done well, and fruitfully done, whatever the world may say or think about it. So that in order that a man may be happy, it is necessary that he should not only be capable of his work, but a good judge of his work.
—John Ruskin

DON'T CONDESCEND TO unskilled labor. Try it for half a day first.
—Brooks Atkinson

WHEN YOUR WORK speaks for itself, don't interrupt.
—Henry J. Kaiser

DON'T TRY TO master too many things.
—William McKinley

IF YOU WOULD be remembered, do one thing superbly well.
—Saunders Norvell

Career

WOMEN ARE TOLD today they can have it all—career, marriage, children. You need a total commitment to make it work. Take a close look at your child. He doesn't want to be bright, talented, chic or smart—any of those things. He just wants you to love him. He will be the one who pays the price for your wanting to have it all. . . . There are two keys: one, believe in yourself; two, love. You must ooze it from every pore. Love your work, your husband and your child, not just to hear his needs but to feel his needs. For your husband you must reserve that thirtieth hour of the day when he has you all alone to himself. If you wonder when you'll get time to rest, well, you can sleep in your old age if you live that long.

—Beverly Sills

ONE CANNOT EXPECT to coast along and rise automatically to the top, no matter what friends you may have in the company. There may have been a time when, in large corporations, a person could rise simply because he had a stock interest or because he had friends in top management. That's not true today. Success in business requires training and discipline and hard work. But if you're not frightened by these things, the opportunities are just as great today as they ever were.

—David Rockefeller

WHENEVER IT IS in any way possible, every boy and girl should choose as his life work some occupation which he should like to do anyhow, even if he did not need the money.

—William Lyon Phelps

Caution

MEASURE A THOUSAND times and cut once.

—Turkish proverb

THREE THINGS IT is best to avoid: a strange dog, a flood, and a man who thinks he is wise.

—Welsh proverb

KEEP YOURSELF FROM the anger of a great man, from the tumult of a mob, from a man of ill fame, from a widow that has been thrice married, from a wind that comes in at a hole, and from a reconciled enemy.

—H. G. Bohn

DON'T TAKE THE bull by the horns, take him by the tail; then you can let go when you want to.

—Josh Billings

NISI CASTE, SALTEM CAUTE. (If not chastely, then at least cautiously.)

—Latin proverb

NEVER PLAY CARDS with a man named Doc. Never eat at a place called Mom's. Never sleep with a woman whose troubles are worse than your own.

—Nelson Algren

Change

KEEP CONSTANTLY IN mind in how many things you yourself have witnessed changes already. The universe is change, life is understanding.

—Marcus Aurelius

THE DOGMAS OF the quiet past are inadequate to the stormy present. The occasion is piled high with difficulty, and we must rise with the occasion. As our case is new, so we must think anew and act anew. We must disenthrall ourselves.

—Abraham Lincoln

THE PROBLEM IS not therefore, to suppress change, which cannot be done, but to manage it. If we opt for rapid change in certain sectors of life we can consciously attempt to build stability zones elsewhere. A divorce perhaps, should not be too closely followed by a job transfer . . . the recent widow should not, perhaps, rush to sell her house.

—Alvin Toffler

KEEP CHANGING. WHEN you're through changing, you're through.

—Bruce Barton

CHANGE NOT THE mass but change the fabric of your own soul and your own visions, and you change all.

—Vachel Lindsay

ONE MUST NEVER lose time in vainly regretting the past nor in complaining about the changes which cause us discomfort, for change is the very essence of life.

—Anatole France

ALTER YOUR MANNER of life ten times if you wish. —Llewelyn Powys

THERE IS NO way to make people like change. You can only make them feel less threatened by it.

—Frederick O'R. Hayes

Character

YOU CANNOT DREAM yourself into a character; you must hammer and forge yourself one.

—James A. Froude

IN ATTEMPTS TO improve your character, know what is in your power and what is beyond it.

—Francis Thompson

IF YOU THINK about what you ought to do for other people, your character will take care of itself.

—Woodrow Wilson

NO MATTER HOW full a reservoir of *maxims* one may possess, and no matter how good one's *sentiments* may be, if one has not taken advantage of every concrete opportunity to *act,* one's character may remain entirely unaffected for the better.

—William James

Sow a thought, reap an act;
Sow an act, reap a habit;
Sow a habit, reap a character;
Sow a character, reap a destiny.

—Anonymous

WHAT YOU WANT to be eventually, that you must be every day; and by and by the quality of your deeds will get down into your soul.

—Frank Crane

IF YOU HEAR that a mountain has moved, believe; but if you hear that a man has changed his character, believe it not. —Mohammedan proverb

PUT MORE TRUST in nobility of character than in an oath. —Solon

Charity

WHEN FAITH AND hope fail, as they do sometimes, we must try charity, which is love in action. We must speculate no more on our duty, but simply do it.
—Dinah Maria Mulock

> Then gently scan your brother, man
> Still gentler sister woman;
> Tho' they may gang a kennin wrang,
> To step aside is human.
>
> —Robert Burns

YOU MUST GIVE some time to your fellow men. Even if it's a little thing, do something for others—something for which you get no pay but the privilege of doing it. —Albert Schweitzer

> He only judges right who weighs, compares
> And, in the sternest sentence which his voice
> Pronounces, ne'er abandons charity.
>
> —William Wordsworth

Cheerfulness

THE BEST WAY to cheer yourself up is to try to cheer somebody else up.

—Mark Twain

LET US BE of good cheer, remembering that the misfortunes hardest to bear are those which never happen. —James Russell Lowell

IF YOU COMMAND wisely, you'll be obeyed cheerfully. —Thomas Fuller

THERE'S MORE TO it than looking your best. You have to be at your best, too—bopping along all the time, happy, upbeat, friendly. —Farrah Fawcett

Children

DON'T SET YOUR wit against a child. —Jonathan Swift

PRAISE THE CHILD, and you make love to the mother. —William Cobbett

GIVE A LITTLE love to a child, and you get a great deal back. —John Ruskin

NE PUERO GLADIUM. (Never give a child a sword.) —Latin proverb

A CHILD . . . SHOULD be pushed aside with the left hand and drawn closer with the right hand. —Babylonian Talmud, tractate Sotah

THERE ARE MANY little ways to enlarge [your child's] world. Love of books is the best of all. —Jacqueline Kennedy Onassis

IF YOU LOVE your son, give him plenty of cudgel; if you hate him, cram him with dainties.

—Chinese proverb

IF YOU STRIKE a child, strike him only with a shoelace.

—Babylonian Talmud, tractate Bava Batra

JUST THINK OF the tragedy of teaching children not to doubt.—Clarence Darrow

LEVEL WITH YOUR child by being honest. Nobody spots a phony quicker than a child.

—Mary MacCracken

I HAVE FOUND the best way to give advice to your children is to find out what they want and then advise them to do it.

—Harry S Truman

GIVE TO A pig when it grunts and a child when it cries, and you will have a fine pig and a bad child.

—Danish proverb

ALLOW CHILDREN TO be happy their own way: for what better way will they ever find?

—Samuel Johnson

NEVER TEACH YOUR child to be cunning for you may be certain you will be one of the very first victims of his shrewdness.

—Josh Billings

DO NOT TRY to produce an ideal child; it would find no fitness in this world.

—Herbert Spencer

IF YOU MUST hold yourself up to your children as an object lesson, hold yourself up as a warning and not as an example.

—George Bernard Shaw

Cleanliness

RESPECT FOR GOD demands that the face, the hands and the feet be washed once a day.
—The Talmud

LET IT BE observed, that slovenliness is no part of religion; that neither this nor any text of Scripture, condemns neatness of apparel. Certainly this is a duty, not a sin. "Cleanliness is, indeed, next to godliness."
—John Wesley

Let thy mind's sweetness have its operation
Upon thy body, clothes and habitation.

—George Herbert

CLEANLINESS AND ORDER are not matters of instinct; they are matters of education, and like most great things—mathematics and classics—you must cultivate a taste for them.
—Benjamin Disraeli

WASH YOUR HANDS always before you come to school. —William Mather, 1681

Commandments

LET US HEAR the conclusion of the whole matter: Fear God, and keep his commandments; for this is the whole duty of man.
—Ecclesiastes, 12

THE TEN COMMANDMENTS:

Thou shalt have no other gods before me.
Thou shalt not make unto thee any graven image, or any likeness of any thing

that is in heaven above, or that is in the earth beneath, or that is in the water under the earth;

Thou shalt not bow down thyself to them, nor see them: for I the Lord thy God am a jealous God, visiting the iniquity of the fathers upon the children unto the third and fourth generation of them that hate me; And shewing mercy unto thousands of them that love me and keep my commandments.

Thou shalt not take the name of the Lord thy God in vain; for the Lord will not hold him guiltless that taketh his name in vain.

Remember the sabbath day, to keep it holy. Six days shalt thou labour, and do all thy work: But the seventh day is the sabbath of the Lord thy God: in it thou shalt not do any work, thou, nor thy son, nor thy daughter, thy manservant, nor thy maidservant, nor thy cattle, nor thy stranger that is within thy gates; For in six days the Lord made heaven and earth, the sea, and all that in them is, and rested the seventh day: wherefore the Lord blessed the sabbath day, and hallowed it.

Honour thy father and thy mother: that thy days may be long upon the land which the Lord thy God giveth thee.

Thou shalt not kill.

Thou shalt not commit adultery.

Thou shalt not bear false witness against thy neighbour.

Thou shalt not covet thy neighbour's house, thou shalt not covet thy neighbour's wife, nor his manservant, nor his maidservant, nor his ox, nor his ass, nor any thing that is thy neighbour's. —Exodus, 20

LIVE BY THE commandments; do not die by them. —The Talmud, Sanhedrin

Commitment

IF YOU START to take Vienna—take Vienna.

—Napoleon Bonaparte

TO FIGHT OUT a war, you must believe something and want something with all your might. So must you do to carry anything else to an end worth reaching. More than that, you must be willing to commit yourself to a course, perhaps a long and hard one, without being able to foresee exactly where you will come out.

—Oliver Wendell Holmes, Jr.

Communication

THINK LIKE A wise man but communicate in the language of the people.

—William Butler Yeats

PUT IT BEFORE them briefly so they will read it, clearly so they will appreciate it, picturesquely so they will remember it and, above all, accurately so they will be guided by its light.

—Joseph Pulitzer

NEVER WRITE ON a subject without first having read yourself full on it; and never read on a subject till you have thought yourself hungry on it.

—Jean Paul Richter

I ATTRIBUTE THE little I know to my not having been ashamed to ask for information and to my rule of conversing with all descriptions of men on those topics that form their own peculiar professions and pursuits.

—John Locke

Communication (Personal)

LIFE IS SHORT and we never have enough time for gladdening the hearts of those who travel the way with us. O, be swift to love! Make haste to be kind.

—Henri F. Amiel

If you have a friend worth loving,
    Love him. Yes, and let him know
That you love him, ere life's evening
    Tinge his brow with sunset glow.
Why should good words ne'er be said
Of a friend till he is dead?

—Daniel W. Hoyt

IF YOU LOVE me, let it appear.

—Saint Augustine

TALK NOT OF wasted affection! Affection never was wasted. . . .

—Henry Wadsworth Longfellow

Companions

ASSOCIATE YOURSELF WITH men of good quality if you esteem your own reputation for 'tis better to be alone than in bad company. —George Washington

BE VERY CIRCUMSPECT in the choice of thy company. In the society of thine equals thou shalt enjoy more pleasure; in the society of thy superiors thou shalt find more profit. To be the best in the company is the way to grow worse; the best means to grow better is to be the worst there. —Francis Quarles

A MAN SHOULD live with his superiors as he does with his fire; not too near, lest he burn; nor too far off, lest he freeze. —Diogenes

FORSAKE NOT AN old friend; for the new is not comparable to him: a new friend is as new wine; when it is old, thou shalt drink it with pleasure.

—Old Testament

BETTER FARE HARD with good men than feast it with bad. —Thomas Fuller

Competition

THE MOST IMPORTANT thing in the Olympic Games is not winning but taking part. . . . The essential thing in life is not conquering but fighting well.

—Baron Pierre de Coubertin,

founder of the modern Olympic Games

IF YOU DON'T try to win you might as well hold the Olympics in somebody's back yard. The thrill of competing carries with it the thrill of a gold medal. One wants to win to prove himself the best. —Jesse Owens

ALWAYS IMITATE THE behavior of the winners when you lose. —Anonymous

IN LIFE, AS in a football game, the principle to follow is: Hit the line hard.

—Theodore Roosevelt

WHEN [TY] COBB got on first base he had an apparently nervous habit of kicking the bag. It wasn't until he retired from the game that the secret came out. By kicking the bag hard enough Cobb could move it a full two inches closer to second base. He figured that this improved his chances for a steal or for reaching second base safely on a hit. Compete, compete, compete—this is the keep-it-going spirit by which the person who tries will ultimately make records.

—Norman Vincent Peale

IF YOU CAN'T win, make the fellow ahead of you break the record.

—Anonymous

Complaint

COMPLAIN TO ONE who can help you. —Yugoslav proverb

LEARN TO ACCEPT in silence the minor aggravations, cultivate the gift of taciturnity, and consume your own smoke with an extra draft of hard work, so that those about you may not be annoyed with the dust and soot of your complaints.

—Sir William Osler

OBTAIN FROM YOURSELF all that makes complaining useless. No longer implore from others what you yourself can obtain. —André Gide

Complexes/Anxiety

BETTER BE DESPISED for too anxious apprehensions, than ruined by too confident security. —Edmund Burke

A MAN SHOULD not strive to eliminate his complexes but to get into accord with them; they are legitimately what directs his conduct in the world.

—Sigmund Freud

BORROW TROUBLE FOR yourself, if that's your nature, but don't lend it to your neighbors. —Rudyard Kipling

WORRY A LITTLE bit every day and in a lifetime you will lose a couple of years. If something is wrong, fix it if you can. But train yourself not to worry. Worry never fixes anything.
—Mary (Mrs. Ernest) Hemingway

Compliments

LEARN HOW TO pay compliments. Start with the members of your family, and you will find it will become easier later in life to compliment others. It's a great asset.
—Letitia Baldrige

DON'T TELL A woman she's pretty; tell her there's no other woman like her, and all roads will open to you.
—Jules Renard

WHEN YOU CANNOT get a compliment any other way pay yourself one.
—Mark Twain

THE BEST WAY to turn a woman's head is to tell her she has a beautiful profile.
—Sacha Guitry

WHEN YOU DON'T know much about a subject you're explaining, compliment the person you are explaining to on knowing all about it and he will think that you do, too.
—Don Marquis

Concentration

BEWARE OF DISSIPATING your powers; strive constantly to concentrate them. Genius thinks it can do whatever it sees others doing, but is sure to repent of every ill-judged outlay.
—Goethe

IF YOU WOULD be pope, you must think of nothing else.   —Spanish proverb

HE ALSO TAUGHT me by his example that the key to music, the key to life, is concentration. —Bobby Hackett, trumpeter, about Louis Armstrong

THE FIELD OF consciousness is tiny. It accepts only one problem at a time. Get into a fist fight, put your mind on the strategy of the fight, and you will not feel the other fellow's punches. —Antoine de Saint-Exupéry

ONE SHOULD ALWAYS think of what one is about; when one is learning, one should not think of play; and when one is at play, one should not think of one's learning. —Lord Chesterfield

DON'T TRY TO do two or more things at once. Set priorities so that you are not worrying about something else while you are attending to the task at hand. Arrange your work space so that your eyes aren't drawn to other jobs that need to be done. The time you invest to organize your space will be paid back with improved efficiency. Don't put unreasonable demands on your attention span. . . . Even if you are under pressure, time spent taking a regular break will increase your overall productivity. But make it a real break; don't just switch to another demanding task. . . . Lack of sleep is a major reason for poor concentration. Learn to take catnaps or use a meditation technique instead of a drug to help you to keep going until you get a good night's rest. —William Bennett, M.D.

Conciseness

IF YOU WOULD be pungent, be brief; for it is with words as with sunbeams— the more they are condensed, the deeper they burn. —Robert Southey

When you've got a thing to say,
Say it! Don't take half a day.

When your tale's got little in it,
Crowd the whole thing in a minute!

—Joel Chandler Harris

NEVER BE SO brief as to become obscure.

—Tryon Edwards

VIGOROUS WRITING IS concise. A sentence should contain no unnecessary words, a paragraph no unnecessary sentences, for the same reason that a drawing should have no unnecessary lines and a machine no unnecessary parts. This requires not that the writer make all his sentences short, or that he avoid all detail and treat his subjects only in outline, but that every word tell.

—William Strunk

AS REPORTERS WE were supposed to tell the news as succinctly and objectively as possible. But it's not always appropriate for a novelist or a playwright or an advertising copywriter, a public relations specialist or a consumer affairs professional. For the job of the novelist and the playwright is to entertain and our job in corporate communications is to convince, and, if necessary, proselytize. To entertain and to convince you need more than clarity. You need eloquence. You need flair. You need the whole gamut of words and sentence structures—the involved and the complex as well as the bare bones simple.

—Melvin J. Grayson

Conduct

There, my blessing with thee!
And these few precepts in thy memory
Look thou character. Give thy thoughts no tongue

Nor any unproportion'd thought his act.
Be thou familiar, but by no means vulgar.

—Polonius, in Shakespeare's
Hamlet Prince of Denmark

MAKE YOURSELF NECESSARY to somebody. Do not make life hard to any.

—Ralph Waldo Emerson

BE NEITHER TOO remote nor too familiar.   —Charles, Prince of Wales

BE CIVIL TO all; sociable to many; familiar with few; friend to one; enemy to none.

—Benjamin Franklin

DON'T BE TOO sweet, lest you be eaten up; don't be too bitter, lest you be spewed out.

—Jewish proverb

MY CODE OF life and conduct is simply this; work hard; play to the allowable limit; disregard equally the good and bad opinion of others; never do a friend a dirty trick; . . . never grow indignant over anything; . . . live the moment to the utmost of its possibilities; . . . and be satisfied with life always, but never with oneself.

—George Jean Nathan

Confidence

THERE ARE ADMIRABLE potentialities in every human being. Believe in your strength and your youth. Learn to repeat endlessly to yourself. "It all depends on me."

—André Gide

DO CONTINUE TO believe that with your feeling and your work you are taking part in the *greatest;* the more strongly you cultivate in yourself this belief, the more will reality and the world go forth from it. —Rainer Maria Rilke

IF YOU DOUBT you can accomplish something, then you can't accomplish it. You have to have confidence in your ability, and then be tough enough to follow through. —Rosalynn Carter

> Go to your bosom;
> Knock there, and ask your heart what it doth know.
> —Isabella, in Shakespeare's
> *Measure for Measure*

Conscience

LABOR TO KEEP alive in your breast that little spark of celestial fire called conscience. —George Washington

IN THE MIDST of all the doubts which we have discussed for four thousand years in four thousand ways, the safest course is to do nothing against one's conscience. With this secret, we can enjoy life and have no fear from death. —Voltaire

TRUST THAT MAN in nothing who has not a conscience in everything. —Laurence Sterne

. . . GOLF HAS A history of conscience. . . . The late Babe Didrikson Zaharias once disqualified herself from a tournament for having hit the wrong ball out of the rough. "But nobody would have known," a friend told her. "I would've known," Babe Didrikson Zaharias replied. Too many people in sports do not understand that now.

—Dave Anderson

Consideration/ Thoughtfulness

ALWAYS BE NICE to people on the way up; because you'll meet the same people on the way down.

—Wilson Mizner

IF YOU TREAT people right they will treat you right—ninety percent of the time.

—Franklin D. Roosevelt

WIN HEARTS, AND you have all men's hands and purses.—William Cecil Burleigh

> Among those who stand, do not sit;
> among those who sit, do not stand.
> Among those who laugh, do not weep;
> among those who weep, do not laugh.

—Jewish proverb

IF YOU CANNOT lift the load off another's back, do not walk away. Try to lighten it.

—Frank Tyger

DO NOT APPEASE your fellow in his hour of anger; do not comfort him while the dead is still laid out before him; do not question him in the hour of his vow; and do not strive to see him in his hour of misfortune.—Rabbi Simeon ben Eleazar

THINK TWICE BEFORE you speak to a friend in need.

—Ambrose Bierce

Consistency

A FOOLISH CONSISTENCY is the hobgoblin of little minds, adored by little statesmen and philosophers and divines. With consistency a great soul has simply nothing to do. . . . Speak what you think now in hard words and to-morrow speak what to-morrow thinks in hard words again, though it contradict every thing you said to-day.
—Ralph Waldo Emerson

DON'T BE ''CONSISTENT,'' but be simply true.
—Oliver Wendell Holmes

Some positive, persisting fops we know,
Who, if once wrong, will needs be always so;
But you with pleasure own your errors past
And make each day a critique on the last.

—Alexander Pope

Contention

NEVER CONTEND WITH a man who has nothing to lose.
—Baltasar Gracian

THE BEST ARMOR is to keep out of range.
—Italian proverb

WHOEVER BATTLES WITH monsters had better see that it does not turn him into a monster. And if you gaze long into an abyss, the abyss will gaze back at you.
—Friedrich Nietzsche

ABOVE ALL THINGS, never be afraid. The enemy who forces you to retreat is himself afraid of you at that very moment.
—André Maurois

YOU DON'T LEARN to hold your own in the world by standing on guard, but by attacking, and getting well-hammered yourself.   —George Bernard Shaw

DON'T HIT AT all if it is honorably possible to avoid hitting; but *never* hit soft!
—Theodore Roosevelt

NEVER CONTEND WITH one that is foolish, proud, positive, testy, or with a superior, or a clown, in matter of argument.   —Thomas Fuller

. . . GO AFTER A man's weakness, and never, ever, threaten unless you're going to follow through, because if you don't, the next time you won't be taken seriously.   —Roy M. Cohn

WHEN YOU MEET your antagonist, do everything in a mild and agreeable manner. Let your courage be as keen, but at the same time as polished, as your sword.   —Richard Brinsley Sheridan

KEEP YOUR BROKEN arm inside your sleeve.   —Chinese proverb

DO NOT THROW the arrow which will return against you.   —Kurdish proverb

Contentment

ENJOY YOUR OWN life without comparing it with that of another.
—Marquis de Condorcet

DO NOT DESPISE your situation; in it you must act, suffer and conquer. From every point on earth we are equally near to heaven and to the infinite.
—Henri F. Amiel

REFLECT ON YOUR present blessings, of which every man has many, not on your past misfortunes, of which all men have some. —Charles Dickens

DO NOT SPOIL what you have by desiring what you have not; but remember that what you now have was once among the things only hoped for.—Epicurus

IT IS BETTER to follow even the shadow of the best than to remain content with the worst. And those who would see wonderful things must often be ready to travel alone. —Henry Van Dyke

BE CONTENTED WHEN you have got all you want. —Holbrook Jackson

BE CONTENT WITH your lot; one cannot be first in everything. —Aesop

ONE SHOULD EITHER be sad or joyful. Contentment is a warm sty for eaters and sleepers. —Eugene O'Neill

I HAVE A simple philosophy. Fill what's empty. Empty what's full. And scratch where it itches. —Alice Roosevelt Longworth

Conversation

TAKE AS MANY half minutes as you can get, but never talk more than half a minute without pausing and giving others an opportunity to strike in.

ONE OF THE best rules in conversation is, never to say a thing which any of the company can reasonably wish had been left unsaid. —Jonathan Swift

SET YOUR FACE against cliches, against fad phrases—and vow to express a thought in your own words instead. . . . Don't dress a simple idea in complicated language. . . . Good conversation is what makes us interesting. After all, we spend a great deal of our time talking and a great deal of our time listening. Why be bored, why be boring—when you don't have to be either.

—Edwin Newman

Don't tell your friends about your indigestion.
"How are you" is a greeting, not a question.

—Arthur Guiterman

IF YOU ARE telling a joke, don't ask people if they've heard it before.

—Sheila Ostrander

DON'T KEEP JINGLING in the course of your conversation any intellectual money you may have.

—Joseph Farrell

IN CONVERSATION USE some, but not too much ceremony; it teaches others to be courteous, too.

—Thomas Fuller

TRUMPET IN A herd of elephants; crow in the company of cocks; bleat in a flock of goats.

—Malayan proverb

IF YOU EXPLORE beneath shyness or party chit-chat, you can sometimes turn a dull exchange into an intriguing one. I've found this to be particularly true in the case of professors or intellectuals, who are full of fascinating information, but need encouragement before they'll divulge it.

—Joyce Carol Oates

AVOID BREAKING INTO a small group engaged in earnest conversation. Cultivate a sense of the fitness of things.

—Jean Carpenter Hall

THE TIME TO stop talking is when the other person nods his head affirmatively but says nothing.
—Henry S. Haskins

Convictions

I'D LIKE TO reverse a traditional piece of commencement time advice. You know it well, it goes: "Make no little plans." Instead, I'd like to say this: Make no little enemies—people with whom you differ for some petty, insignificant, personal reason. Instead, I would urge you to cultivate "mighty opposites"—people with whom you disagree on big issues, with whom you will fight to the end over fundamental convictions. And that fight, I can assure you, will be good for you and your opponent.
—Thomas J. Watson, Jr.

REMEMBER THAT WHAT you believe will depend very much on what you are.
—Noah Porter

ONE NEEDS TO be slow to form convictions, but once formed they must be defended against the heaviest odds.
—Mohandas K. Gandhi

EVEN WHEN YOU are sure, seem rather doubtful; and, if you would convince others, seem open to conviction yourself.
—Lord Chesterfield

Coping

[A] WORKABLE AND effective way to meet and overcome difficulties is to take on someone else's problems. It is a strange fact, but you can often handle two difficulties—your own and somebody else's—better than you can handle your own alone. That truth is based on a subtle law of self-giving or outgoingness whereby you develop a self-strengthening in the process.—Norman Vincent Peale

Let us be patient! These severe afflictions
Not from the ground arise,
But oftentimes celestial benedictions
Assume this dark disguise.

—Henry Wadsworth Longfellow

DON'T LET YOUR sorrow come higher than your knees. —Swedish proverb

Counsel

CONSULT YOUR FRIEND on all things, especially on those which respect yourself. His counsel may then be useful when your own self-love might impair your judgment. —Seneca

IN GIVING ADVICE, seek to help, not please, your friend. —Solon

LET NO MAN value at a little price a virtuous woman's counsel.—George Chapman

THE ADVICE OF friends must be received with a judicious reserve; we must not give ourselves up to it and follow it blindly, whether right or wrong.

—Pierre Charron

REMEMBER THAT COMMENT, however judicious, is not advice; and that advice should always tend to something practicable. —Sir Arthur Helps

NEVER TAKE THE advice of someone who has not had your kind of trouble.

—Sidney J. Harris

NEVER TRUST THE advice of a man in difficulties. —Aesop

DO NOT OFFER advice which has not been seasoned by your own performance. —Henry S. Haskins

IF YOU WANT a man to resolve upon following your advice, speak to him kindly. —Jean Guibert

PEOPLE WHO ASK our advice almost never take it. Yet we should never refuse to give it, upon request, for it often helps us to see our own way more clearly. —Brendan Francis

AS TO ADVICE, be wary: if it is honest, it is also criticism. —David Grayson

NEVER ADVISE ANYONE to go to war or to marry. —Spanish proverb

NEVER GIVE ADVICE unless asked. —German proverb

ASK ADVICE ONLY of your equals. —Danish proverb

(*See also* Bad Advice, Facetious Advice, Questionable Advice, and Fatherly Advice.)

Courage

ONE OUGHT NEVER to turn one's back on a threatened danger and try to run away from it. If you do that, you will double the danger. But if you meet it promptly and without flinching, you will reduce the danger by half. Never run away from anything. Never! —Sir Winston Churchill

YOU CANNOT RUN away from a weakness; you must sometimes fight it out or perish. And if that be so, why not now, and where you stand? —Robert Louis Stevenson

BEING A MAN, ne'er ask the gods for a life set free from grief, but ask for courage that endureth long.

—Menander

HAVE COURAGE FOR the great sorrows of life and patience for the small ones; and when you have laboriously accomplished your daily task, go to sleep in peace. God is awake.

—Victor Hugo

LIVE AS BRAVE men; and if fortune is adverse, front its blows with brave hearts.

—Cicero

YOU HAVE GOT to have courage. I don't care how good a man is, if he is timid, his value is limited. The timid will not amount to very much in this world. I want to see a good man ready to smite with the sword. I want to see him able to hold his own in active life against the force of evil.

—Theodore Roosevelt

TELL A MAN he is brave, and you help him to become so.

—Thomas Carlyle

WHEN IN DOUBT, do the courageous thing.

—Jan Smuts

FALL SEVEN TIMES, stand up eight.

—Japanese proverb

He that climbs the tall tree has won right to the fruit.
He that leaps the wide gulf should prevail in his suit.

—Sir Walter Scott

A LOT OF my philosophy comes from the ring. You learn in life there are always the ups and downs. We must have enough sense to enjoy our ups and enough heart to get through our downs.

—Mickey Walker

Courtesy/Propriety

ALWAYS BEHAVE AS if nothing had happened no matter what has happened.
—Arnold Bennett

AVOID ALL SINGULARITY and affectation. What is according to nature is best, while what is contrary to it is always distasteful. Nothing is graceful that is not our own.
—Jeremy Collier

WHEN YOU ARE in Rome live in the Roman style; when you are elsewhere live as they live elsewhere.
—Saint Ambrose, advice to Saint Augustine

COMPORT THYSELF IN life as at a banquet. If a plate is offered thee, extend thy hand and take it moderately; if it is to be withdrawn, do not detain it. If it come to thy side, make not thy desire loudly known, but wait patiently until it be offered thee.
—Epictetus

IF YOU BOW at all, bow low.
—Chinese proverb

THE GREAT SECRET, Eliza, is not a question of good manners, or bad manners or any particular sort of manners, but having the same manner for all human souls. The question is not whether I treat you rudely, but whether you have heard me treat anyone else better.
—Henry Higgins, in Lerner and Loewe's
My Fair Lady, based on Shaw's *Pygmalion*

Creativity

IF YOU WOULD create something, you must be something. —Goethe

BE BRAVE ENOUGH to live life creatively. The creative is the place where no one else has ever been. You have to leave the city of your comfort and go into the wilderness of your intuition. You can't get there by bus, only by hard work and risk and by not quite knowing what you're doing. What you'll discover will be wonderful. What you'll discover will be yourself.

—Alan Alda, advice to his daughter

TAKE AN OBJECT. Do something to it. Do something else to it. —Jasper Johns

IN THE MODERN world of business, it is useless to be a creative original thinker unless you can also sell what you create. Management cannot be expected to recognize a good idea unless it is presented to them by a good salesman.

—David M. Ogilvy

WHEN ALEXANDER THE GREAT visited Diogenes and asked whether he could do anything for the famed teacher, Diogenes replied: "Only stand out of my light." Perhaps some day we shall know how to heighten creativity. Until then, one of the best things we can do for creative men and women is to stand out of their light.

—John W. Gardner

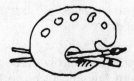

Crime

IF YOU HAVE committed iniquity, you must expect to suffer; for vengeance with its sacred light shines upon you.

—Sophocles

DO NOT ENVY a sinner; you don't know what disaster awaits him.

—Old Testament

THERE IS NO den in the wide world to hide a rogue. Commit a crime and the earth is made of glass. Commit a crime, and it seems as if a coat of snow fell on the ground, such as reveals in the woods the track of every partridge, and fox, and squirrel.

—Ralph Waldo Emerson

TAKE OFF THE strong cord of discipline and morality, and you will be an old man before your twenties are past. Preserve these forces. Do not burn them out in idleness or crime.

—James A. Garfield

SET A THIEF to catch a thief.

—French proverb

Criticism

SPEAK THE TRUTH by all means; be bold and fearless in your rebuke of error, and in your keener rebuke of wrongdoing; but be human, and loving, and gentle, and brotherly, the while.

—W. N. Punshon

BE NOT AFFRONTED at a jest; if one throw ever so much salt at thee thou wilt receive no harm unless thou art raw and ulcerous.

—Junius

Fear not the anger of the wise to raise;
Those best can bear reproof who merit praise.

—Alexander Pope

WHEN A MAN tells you what people are saying about you, tell him what people are saying about him; that will immediately take his mind off your troubles.

—E. W. Howe

REPROVE THY FRIEND privately; commend him publicly.   —Solon

DO NOT REMOVE a fly from your friend's forehead with a hatchet.

—Chinese proverb

THE RULE IN carving holds good as to criticism; never cut with a knife what you can cut with a spoon.   —Charles Buxton

WE SHOULD BE modest and circumspect in expressing an opinion on the conduct of such eminent men, lest we fall into the common error of condemning what we do not understand.   —Marcus Fabius Quintilianus

ALWAYS KEEP IN mind the part that mood can play in affecting one's judgment of a piece of work; be cautious of enthusiasm when the sun shines bright, and slow to dismissal when the clouds hang low.   —J. Donald Adams

YOU SHOULD NOT say it is not good. You should say you do not like it; and then, you know, you're perfectly safe.   —James McNeill Whistler

NEVER JUDGE A work of art by its defects.   —Washington Allston

REFRAIN FROM CORRECTING a friend's misuse or mispronunciation of a word in the presence of others. If he says "integrate" when he means "correlate"—let it go! If you correct him publicly, you draw attention to his mistake and embarrass him.
—Lillian Eichler Watson

REST SATISFIED WITH doing well, and leave others to talk of you as they please.
—Pythagoras

(*See also* Praise.)

Curiosity

SEIZE THE MOMENT of excited curiosity on any subject to solve your doubts; for if you let it pass, the desire may never return, and you may remain in ignorance.
—William Wirt

THE IMPORTANT THING is not to stop questioning. Curiosity has its own reason for existing. One cannot help but be in awe when he contemplates the mysteries of eternity, of life, of the marvelous structure of reality. It is enough if one tries merely to comprehend a little of this mystery every day. Never lose a holy curiosity.
—Albert Einstein

LIFE WAS MEANT to be lived, and curiosity must be kept alive. One must never, for whatever reason, turn his back on life.
—Eleanor Roosevelt

Cynicism

DON'T BE CYNICAL. . . . There'll be deaths and disappointments and failures. When they come, you meet them. Nobody promises you a good time or an easy time. I don't know who it was who said when we think of the past we

regret and we think of the future we fear. And with reason. There are no bets on it. There is the present to think of, and as long as you live there always will be. In the present, every day is a miracle.
—James Gould Cozzens

NEVER, NEVER, NEVER be a cynic, even a gentle one. Never help out a sneer, even at the devil.
—Vachel Lindsay

DON'T BE A cynic and bewail and bemoan. Omit the negative propositions. Don't waste yourself in rejection, nor bark against the bad, but chant the beauty of the good.
—Ralph Waldo Emerson

OPEN YOUR EYES! The world is still intact.
—Paul Claudel

DANCE · DANGER · DARING · DAY · DEATH · DECISION

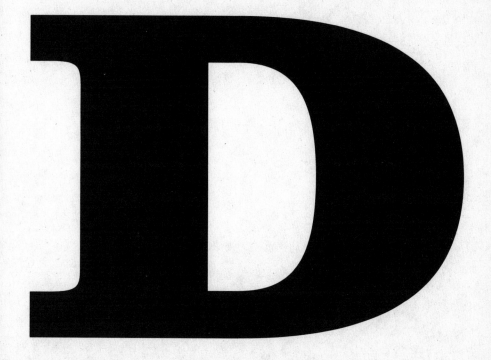

DEDICATION · DESPAIR · DETERMINATION · DIFFICULTIES · DINING/ENTERAINING

Dance

WITHOUT DANCING YOU can never attain a perfectly graceful carriage, which is of the highest importance in life.

—Benjamin Disraeli

DANCING IZ AN excellent amusement for yung people, especially for those of sedentary occupations. Its excellence consists in exciting a cheerfulness of the mind, highly essential to helth; in bracing the muscles of the body, and in producing copious perspiration. . . . The body must perspire, or must be out of order.

—Noah Webster (in reformed spelling)

On with the dance! Let joy be unconfined;
No sleep till morn, when Youth and Pleasure meet
To chase the glowing Hours with flying feet.

—Lord Byron

Danger

LET THE FEAR of a danger be a spur to prevent it; he that fears not, gives advantage to the danger. —Francis Quarles

NEVER EXPOSE YOURSELF unnecessarily to danger; a miracle may not save you . . . and if it does, it will be deducted from your share of luck or merit. —The Talmud

DON'T PLAY FOR safety. It's the most dangerous thing in the world. —Hugh Walpole

PUT YOUR TRUST in God—but keep your powder dry. —Oliver Cromwell

IF YOU ARE out of trouble, watch for danger. —Sophocles

AFTER VICTORY, TIGHTEN your helmet cord. —Japanese proverb

Daring

IF YOU GREATLY desire something, have the guts to stake everything on obtaining it. —Brendan Francis

WHY NOT GO out on a limb? Isn't that where the fruit is? —Frank Scully

FAR BETTER IT is to dare mighty things, to win glorious triumphs, even though checkered by failure, than to take rank with those poor spirits who neither enjoy much nor suffer much, because they live in the gray twilight that knows not victory nor defeat. —Theodore Roosevelt

WHEN YOU HAVE no choice, mobilize the spirit of courage.   —Jewish proverb

TEMPORIZE NOT! IT is always injurious.   —Andrew Jackson

Day

CARPE DIEM. (SEIZE the day.)   —Horace

ALWAYS BEGIN ANEW with the day, just as nature does; it is one of the sensible
things that nature does.   —George E. Woodberry

DO NOT SHORTEN the morning by getting up late; look upon it as the quintes-
sence of life, and to a certain extent sacred.   —Arthur Schopenhauer

> Count that day lost whose low-descending sun
> Views from thy hand no worthy action done.
>
> —Anonymous

LET EACH DAY take thoughts for what concerns it, dispose of its own affairs
and respect the day which is to follow, and we shall always be ready.
—Henri F. Amiel

WAIT UNTIL IT is night before saying that it has been a fine day.—French proverb

Death

DO NOT SEEK death. Death will find you. But seek the road which makes death
a fulfillment.   —Dag Hammarskjold

BE SURE TO send a lazy man for the angel of death.   —Jewish proverb

WHAT YOU LEAVE at your death, let it be without controversy, else the lawyers will be your heirs. —Sir Thomas Browne

IF YOU DO not know how to die, don't worry. Nature herself will teach you in the proper time; she will discharge that work for you; don't trouble yourself.
—Michel de Montaigne

BE OF GOOD hope in the face of death. Believe in this one truth for certain, that no evil can befall a good man either in life or death, and that his fate is not a matter of indifference to the gods. —Socrates

DO NOT FEAR death so much, but rather the inadequate life. —Bertolt Brecht

(*See also* Mortality.)

Decision

Before you begin, get good counsel;
Then, having decided, act promptly.

—Sallust

TAKE TIME TO deliberate, but when the time for action has arrived, stop thinking and go in. —Napoleon Bonaparte

WHEN ONCE A decision is reached and execution is the order of the day, dismiss absolutely all responsibility and care about the outcome.—William James

DON'T BE AFRAID to take a big step when one is indicated. You can't cross a chasm in two small jumps. —David Lloyd George

I leave this rule for others when I'm dead,
Be always sure you're right—then go ahead.

—David Crockett

WHEN A THING is done, it's done. Don't look back. Look forward to your next objective.

—George C. Marshall

FISH OR CUT BAIT.

—American proverb

Dedication

WHATEVER YOUR CAREER may be, do not let yourselves become tainted by a deprecating and barren skepticism, do not let yourself be discouraged by the sadness of certain hours which pass over nations. . . . Say to yourselves first, "What have I done for my instruction?" and as you gradually advance, "What have I done for my country?" until the time comes when you may have the immense happiness of thinking that you have contributed in some way to the progress and to the good of humanity. But whether our efforts are, or not, favored by life, let us be able to say, when we come near to the great goal, "I have done what I could."

—Louis Pasteur

THE ROOTS OF true achievement lie in the will to become the best that you can become.

—Harold Taylor

I ALWAYS REMEMBER an epitaph which is in the cemetery at Tombstone, Arizona. It says: "Here lies Jack Williams. He done his damnedest." I think that is the greatest epitaph a man can have—when he gives everything that is in him to do the job he has before him. That is all you can ask of him and that is what I have tried to do.

—Harry S. Truman

Despair

Beware of desperate steps; the darkest day,
Lived till tomorrow, will have passed away.

—William Cowper

NEVER DESPAIR, BUT if you do, work on in despair. —Edmund Burke

WHEN YOU GET into a tight place and everything goes against you, till it seems you could not hold on a minute longer, never give up then, for that is just the place and time that the tide will turn. —Harriet Beecher Stowe

FACING IT—ALWAYS facing it—that's the way to get through! Face it!

—Joseph Conrad

Determination

IF YOUR DETERMINATION is fixed, I do not counsel you to despair. Few things are impossible to diligence and skill. Great works are performed not by strength, but perseverance. —Samuel Johnson

ALL THAT IS necessary to break the spell of inertia and frustration is this: *Act as if it were impossible to fail.* That is the talisman, the formula, the command of right-about-face which turns us from failure towards success. —Dorothea Brande

Come, my friends,
'Tis not too late to seek a newer world . . .
It may be that the gulfs will wash us down:

It may be we shall touch the Happy Isles,
And see the great Achilles, whom we knew.
Tho' much is taken, much abides; and tho'
We are not now that strength which in old days
Moved earth and heaven; that which we are, we are;
One equal temper of heroic hearts,
Made weak by time and fate, but strong in will
To strive, to seek, to find, and not to yield.

—From Alfred, Lord Tennyson's "Ulysses"

NEVER GIVE UP and never give in.

—Hubert H. Humphrey

GO ON—THE LIMIT!

—John Reed (his creed)

Difficulties

BE OF GOOD courage, all is before you, and time passed in the difficult is never lost. . . . What is required of us is that we love the difficult and learn to deal with it. In the difficult are the friendly forces, the hands that work on us.

—Rainer Maria Rilke

Then welcome each rebuff
That turns earth's smoothness rough,
Each sting that bids not sit nor stand but go!
Be our joys three-parts pain!
Strive and hold cheap the strain;
Learn, nor account the pang; dare, never grudge the throe!

—Robert Browning

WHEN YOU ENCOUNTER difficulties and contradictions, do not try to break them, but bend them with gentleness and time. —Saint Francis de Sales

Dining/Entertaining

THOU SHOULDST EAT to live; not live to eat. —Cicero

ALWAYS REMEMBER IF a friend be dining with one, to help him to the choicest parts. Do not, however, press your friend too warmly to eat or drink, but receive him well, and give him good cheer. —Fra Bonvesin

SPREAD THE TABLE and contention will cease. —English proverb

AT A DINNER party one should eat wisely but not too well, and talk well but not too wisely. —W. Somerset Maugham

AVOID TOO-LARGE red-wine glasses that look like small tubs best used as your gold-fish's permanent home. . . . Don't decant new wines, but if you have the good sense to serve old Port, by all means decant it. . . . Glasses should not be filled to the brim but need more than a splash that looks like a bath prepared for a newborn warbler. —George Lang

NEVER ARGUE AT the dinner table, for the one who is not hungry always gets the best of the argument. —Richard Whately

THE NUMBER OF guests at dinner should not be less than the number of the Graces nor exceed that of the Muses, i.e., it should begin with three and stop at nine. —Varro, a Roman

IF CELEBRITIES ARE among your friends, don't use them to attract people to your parties and don't expect them to be the unpaid entertainment for the evening or to design a dress or redecorate a room over dinner. —Sheila Ostrander

> If you would have guests merry with cheer,
> be so yourself, or so at least appear.
>
> —Benjamin Franklin

Diplomacy

AND ABOVE ALL not too much zeal. —Perigord de Talleyrand

KEEP A GOOD table and look after the ladies. —Napoleon Bonaparte, instructing an ambassador

YOU MIGHT AS well fall flat on your face as lean over too far backwards. —James Thurber

DON'T EVER SLAM the door; you might want to go back. —Don Herold

IF YOU WANT to make peace, you don't talk to your friends. You talk to your enemies. —Moshe Dayan

REMEMBER NOT ONLY to say the right thing in the right place, but far more difficult still, to leave unsaid the wrong thing at the tempting moment. —Benjamin Franklin

Discernment

Give not that which is holy unto the dogs,
Neither cast ye your pearls before swine,
Lest they trample them under their feet,
And turn again and rend you.

Beware of false prophets, which come to you in sheep's clothing,
but inwardly they are ravening wolves.

—Jesus of Nazareth

WHEN YOU SEE a snake, never mind where he came from.　　—W. G. Benham

YOU MUST LOOK into people, as well as at them.　　—Lord Chesterfield

SEE NOT EVIL in others and good in yourself, but the good in the other and the
failings in yourself.
　　　　—The Berdichever Rabbi

Discipline

REMEMBER THE WONDERFUL definition of conscience by Henri Bergson. He
says, "Conscience is memory, attention and anticipation." So, you must bring a
student in music or in anything else to feel that he must remember what he has
seen, see what he sees, and foresee what will follow—what will be there. Then
you develop him not only as a musician but as a man . . . that is the most
important thing to do.
　　　　—Nadia Boulanger

NO PAIN, NO palm; no thorns, no throne; no gall, no glory; no cross, no crown.
—William Penn

> Don't let your heart depend on things
> That ornament life in a fleeting way!
> He who possesses, let him learn to lose,
> He who is fortunate, let him learn pain.
>
> —Johann von Schiller

DO NOT CONSIDER painful what is good for you.
—Euripides

I HAVE ALWAYS adhered to two principles. The first one is to train hard and get into the best possible physical condition. The second is to forget all about the other fellow until you face him in the ring and the bell sounds for the fight.
—Rocky Marciano

Discretion

BE DISCREET IN all things, and so render it unnecessary to be mysterious about any.
—Arthur Wellesley (first Duke of Wellington)

OPEN YOUR MOUTH and purse cautiously, and your stock of wealth and reputation shall, at least in repute, be great.
—Johann Georg von Zimmermann

WHEN YOU HAVE got an elephant by the hind leg, and he is trying to run away, it's best to let him run.
—Abraham Lincoln

IF THOU ART a master, be sometimes blind, if a servant, sometimes deaf.
—Thomas Fuller

THE BETTER PART of valor is discretion, in the which better part I have saved my life.   —Falstaff, in Shakespeare's *The First Part of King Henry IV*

CURSE NOT THE king, no not in thy thought; and curse not the rich in thy bedchamber: for the bird of the air shall carry thy voice, and that which hath wings shall tell the matter.   —Ecclesiastes

Doing

DETERMINE NEVER TO be idle. . . . It is wonderful how much may be done if we are always doing.   —Thomas Jefferson

> Boast not of what thou would'st have done, but do
> What then thou would'st.
>
>   —John Milton

PURSUE, KEEP UP with, circle round and round your life, as a dog does his master's chaise. Do what you love. Know your own bone; gnaw at it, bury it, unearth it, and gnaw it still. . . . If you can drive a nail and have any nails to drive, drive them. Do what you reprove yourself for not doing. Know that you are neither satisfied nor dissatisfied with yourself without reason.   —Henry David Thoreau

IF WE ATTEND continually and promptly to the little that we can do, we shall ere long be surprised to find how little remains that we cannot do.—Samuel Butler

IF YOU'RE ABLE to and want to, then do—for the life to come may be an awful bust.   —William Carlos Williams

Doing Good

Do all the good you can,
In all the ways you can,
In all the places you can,
At all the times you can,
To all the people you can,
As long as ever you can.

—John Wesley

DO DEFINITE GOOD; first of all to yourself, then to definite persons.

—John Lancaster Spalding

DO NOT WAIT for extraordinary situations to do good; try to use ordinary situations.

—Jean Paul Richter

KNOW HOW TO do good a little at a time, and often.

—Baltasar Gracian

LET A GOOD man do good deeds with the same zeal that the evil man does bad ones.

—The Belzer Rabbi

TO BE GOOD, we must do good; and by doing good we take a sure means of being good, as the use and exercise of the muscles increase their power.

—Tryon Edwards

Doubt

IF YOU WOULD be a real seeker after truth, it is necessary that at least once in your life you doubt, as far as possible, all things. —René Descartes

DOUBT 'TIL THOU canst doubt no more . . . doubt is thought and thought is life. Systems which end doubt are devices for drugging thought.—Albert Guérard

MISGIVE, THAT YOU may not mistake. —Richard Whately

DO NOT FIGHT doubts with reasons or with arguments; but fight them with deeds. —Jacques Bénigne Bossuet

NEVER DO ANYTHING concerning the rectitude of which you have a doubt. —Pliny

LET GO THE things in which you are in doubt for the things in which there is no doubt. —Mohammed

WILLIAM JAMES USED to preach the "will to believe." For my part, I should wish to preach the "will to doubt" . . . What is wanted is not the will to believe, but the wish to find out, which is the exact opposite.

IN ALL AFFAIRS it's a healthy thing now and then to hang a question mark on the things you have long taken for granted. —Bertrand Russell

WHEN IN DOUBT, gallop! —French Foreign Legion saying

Dreams

DREAM MANFULLY AND nobly, and thy dreams shall be prophets.

—Edward George Bulwer-Lytton

IF YOU HAVE built castles in the air, your work need not be lost; that is where they should be. Now put the foundations under them. —Henry David Thoreau

REASON MAY FAIL you. If you are going to do anything with life, you have sometimes to move away from it, beyond all measurements. You must follow sometimes visions and dreams. —Bede Jarrett

He ne'er is crowned
With immortality, who fears to follow
Where airy voices lead.

—John Keats

TO ACCOMPLISH GREAT things, we must dream as well as act.—Anatole France

LET NOT OUR babbling dreams affright our souls.—King Richard, in Shakespeare's
The Tragedy of King Richard III

IS LIFE SO wretched? Isn't it rather your hands which are too small, your vision which is muddled? You are the one who must grow up. —Dag Hammarskjold

A SALESMAN IS got to dream, boy. It comes with the territory.

—Willy Loman, in Arthur Miller's
Death of a Salesman

MAKE US, NOT fly to dreams, but moderate desire. —Matthew Arnold

NEVER GROW A wishbone, daughter, where your backbone ought to be.
—Clementine Paddleford

Dress/Fashion

KNOW, FIRST, WHO you are; and then adorn yourself accordingly. —Epictetus

> In clothes as well as speech, the man of sense
> Will shun all the extremes that give offense,
> Dress unaffectedly, and without haste,
> Follow the changes in the current taste.
>
> —Molière

MY FATHER USED to say, "Let them see you and not the suit. That should be secondary." —Cary Grant

UNDER NO CIRCUMSTANCES should any man, whatever size, wear a tight-fitting suit. —Antonio Cristiani

DRESS YOURSELF FINE, where others are fine, and plain, where others are plain; but take care always that your clothes are well made and fit you, for otherwise they will give you a very awkward air. . . . If you are not in fashion, you are nobody. —Lord Chesterfield

BE NEITHER TOO early in the fashion, nor too long out of it, nor too precisely in it. What custom hath civilized is become decent; till then, ridiculous. Where the eye is the jury, thine apparel is the evidence. —Francis Quarles

BEFORE YOU GO out, always take off something you've put on, because you probably are wearing too much.
—Anita Colby

PUT EVEN THE plainest woman into a beautiful dress and unconsciously she will try to live up to it.
—Lady Duff-Gordon

WHEN IN DOUBT, wear red.
—Bill Blass

FORGET ABOUT ''NEAT'' and "meticulous". . . . Don't project "impeccability". . . . If you send out signals of competence and authority, cancel 'em. . . . Be aware of how you look from the back. . . . If you tend toward ethnic dress, look earthy, not poor.
—Barbara Bergdorf with Sue Nirenberg

IF I WERE a young woman with an M.B.A., I think I'd try to keep things conservative.
—Nancy Clark Reynolds

ON DRESS DESIGNING: The trick is timing. You must pick the right idea from the past and use it at the right time in the present.
—Sophie Gimbel

IN YOUR CLOTHES avoid too much gaudiness; do not value yourself upon an embroidered gown; and remember that a reasonable word, or an obliging look, will gain you more respect than all your fine trappings.
—Sir George Savile,
Advice to a Daughter, 1688

Drinking

LOOK CLOSELY AT the people you drink with and see what impact it is having on your drinking. Change drinking partners if you're drinking with people who drink too much.
—Dr. Alan Marlatt

Drink not the third glass—which thou can'st
   not tame
When once it is within thee.

—George Herbert

IF YOU SEE in your wine the reflection of a person not in your range of vision, don't drink it.

—Quoted by George Lang

from a Chinese cookbook

Duty

MAKE IT A point to do something every day that you don't want to do. This is the golden rule for acquiring the habit of doing your duty without pain.

—Mark Twain

WHEN YOU HAVE a number of disagreeable duties to perform, always do the most disagreeable first.

—Josiah Quincy

When Duty comes a-knocking at your gate,
Welcome him in; for if you bid him wait,

He will depart only to come once more
And bring seven other duties to your door.

—Edwin Markham

NEVER MIND YOUR happiness; do your duty.   —Will Durant

KNOWLEDGE OF YOUR duties is the most essential part of the philosophy of life. If you avoid duty, you avoid action. The world demands results.

—George W. Goethals

DO THE DUTY which lieth nearest to thee! Thy second duty will have already become clearer.   —Thomas Carlyle

WE HAVE MOVED from a sense of obligation—of duty—to a sense of entitlement. . . . Everybody appears to deserve a break today except the General Interest. . . . We must learn to moderate our claims to entitlement. We must begin to make the kind of investment of personal time and commitment which will assure that those who come after us will live as well.   —Charles W. Bray III

YOU TOOK THE good things for granted. Now you must earn them again. For every right that you cherish, you have a duty that you must fulfill. For every good which you wish to preserve, you will have to sacrifice your comfort and your ease. There is nothing for nothing any longer.   —Walter Lippmann

DON'T BE MISLED into believing that somehow the world owes you a living. The boy who believes that his parents, or the government, or anyone else owes him a livelihood and that he can collect it without labor will wake up one day and find himself working for another boy who did not have that belief and therefore, earned the right to have others work for him.   —David Sarnoff

D

DUTY THEN IS the sublimest word in our language. Do your duty in all things. You cannot do more. You should never wish to do less. —Robert E. Lee

A PERSON SHOULD do one unpleasant duty a day just to keep himself in moral trim. —William James

DO TODAY'S DUTY . . . and do not weaken and distract yourself by looking forward to things which you cannot see, and could not understand if you saw them. —Charles Kingsley

HOW CAN YOU come to know yourself? Never by thinking, always by doing. Try to do your duty, and you'll know right away what you amount to. And what is your duty? Whatever the day calls for. —Goethe

Eating/Dieting

PREACH NOT TO others what they should eat, but eat as becomes you, and be silent.   —Epictetus

IF HUNGER MAKES you irritable, better eat and be pleasant.   —Sefer Hasidim

> If you wish to grow thinner, diminish your dinner,
> And take to light claret instead of pale ale;
> Look down with utter contempt upon butter,
> And never touch bread till it's toasted—or stale.
>
> —H. S. Leigh

EAT A LOW-CALORIE BALANCED DIET. Fad diets can be dangerous. Manage long-term weight loss under medical supervision.

Change your eating habits and the way you think about food. Permanent weight loss is a lifelong commitment.

Exercise. It burns off the fat and adds muscle tissue.

Don't worry so much about your weight. There's no real evidence that a few 'extra' pounds are harmful.

If, after all the effort, nothing really seems to work for you, don't feel too bad. As one researcher puts it; "There's nothing criminal or immoral in your failure to lose weight."   —From an article in *Business Week*

MAKE HUNGER THY sauce, as a medicine for health.   —Thomas Tusser, 1524

Economy/Debt

IF YOU KNOW how to spend less than you get, you have the philosopher's stone. . . . Beware of little expenses. A small leak will sink a great ship. . . . Ere you consult your fancy, consult your purse. —Benjamin Franklin

> Neither a borrower nor a lender be;
> For loan oft loses both itself and friend,
> And borrowing dulls the edge of husbandry.

—Polonius, in Shakespeare's
Hamlet Prince of Denmark

DO NOT ACCUSTOM yourself to consider debt only as an inconvenience. You will find it a calamity. —Samuel Johnson

ALWAYS PAY; FOR first or last you must pay your entire debt.

—Ralph Waldo Emerson

Education

PERHAPS THE MOST valuable result of all education is the ability to make yourself do the thing you have to do, when it ought to be done, whether you like it or not; it is the first lesson that ought to be learned; and however early a man's training begins, it is probably the last lesson that he learns thoroughly.

—Thomas Henry Huxley

FIRST YOU HAVE to learn something, then you can go out and do it.

—Mies van der Rohe

NEVER REGARD STUDY as a duty, but as the enviable opportunity to learn to know the liberating influence of beauty in the realm of the spirit for your own personal joy and to the profit of the community to which your later work belongs.

—Albert Einstein

IF YOU THINK education is expensive—try ignorance.

—Derek Bok
President, Harvard University

WHEN YOU WISH to instruct, be brief; that men's minds take in quickly what you say, learn its lesson, and retain it faithfully. Every word that is unnecessary only pours over the side of a brimming mind.

—Cicero

IF WE SUCCEED in giving the love of learning, the learning itself is sure to follow.

—John Lubbock

LEARN AS MUCH by writing as by reading.

—Lord Acton

DON'T DESPAIR OF a student if he has one clear idea.

—Nathanial Emmons

LOOK TO THE Classics, History, to the Arts, for there is the truth. Look away from the systems, the processes, the techniques.

—Charles Guggenheim

NEVER DISCOURAGE ANYONE . . . who continually makes progress, no matter how slow.

—Plato

(*See also* Training and Teaching.)

Education (Children)

TRAIN UP A child in the way he should go; and when he is old, he will not depart from it.
— Old Testament

LET THY CHILD'S first lesson be obedience, and the second will be what thou wilt.
— Benjamin Franklin

IN THE EDUCATION of children there is nothing like alluring the interest and affection; otherwise you only make so many asses laden with books.
— Michel de Montaigne

LET EARLY EDUCATION be a sort of amusement; you will then be better able to find out the natural bent.
— Plato

IF, IN INSTRUCTING a child, you are vexed with it for want of adroitness, try, if you have never tried before, to write with your left hand, and then remember that a child is all left hand.
— J. F. Boyse

Education (Young People)

NEVER TEACH FALSE morality. How exquisitely absurd to teach a girl that beauty is of no value, dress of no use! Beauty is of value—her whole prospects and happiness in life may often depend upon a new gown or a becoming bonnet; if she has five grains of common sense, she will find this out. The great thing is to teach her their just value, and that there must be something better under the bonnet than a pretty face, for real happiness. But never sacrifice truth.
— Sydney Smith

TRY TO BE open with your child, allowing her to express her ideas and to confide her experiences and desires. Some of what she says you may find objectionable, but remember that she is struggling to develop herself in an atmosphere that differs considerably from the one in which you grew up. Being open with your child does not mean you must accept whatever she says or does. Indeed, you have an obligation to offer your opinions but it will be more effective if you avoid lecturing or moralizing when you do. —Saul Kapel, M.D.

DON'T LIMIT A child to your own learning, for he was born in another time.
—Rabbinical saying

ABOVE ALL THINGS we must take care that the child, who is not yet old enough to love his studies, does not come to hate them and dread the bitterness which he has once tasted, even when the years of infancy are left behind. His studies must be made an amusement. —Marcus Fabius Quintilianus

Effort

LIFT WHERE YOU stand. —Edward Everett Hale

KEEP THE FACULTY of effort alive in you by a little gratuitous exercise each day. This is, to be systematically ascetic or heroic in little unnecessary points, to do every day or two something for no other reason than that you would rather not do it, so that when the hour of dire need draws nigh, it may find you not unnerved and untrained to stand the test. —William James

IT IS FOR us to make the effort. The result is always in God's hands.
—Mohandas K. Gandhi

THERE IS NO short cut to fame and comfort and all there is is to bore into it as hard as you can. —Oliver Wendell Holmes, Jr.

Emotions

EMOTION: AH! LET us never be one of those who treat lightly one of the words that most deserve reverence. —Charles Du Bos

CHERISH YOUR OWN emotions and never undervalue them. —Robert Henri

IN THE SPHERE of the emotions it is very useful to struggle with the habit of giving immediate expression to all one's unpleasant emotions.—Georges Gurdjieff

THE TASTE FOR emotion may become a dangerous taste; we should be very cautious how we attempt to squeeze out of human life more ecstasy and paroxysm than it can well afford. —Sydney Smith

Endurance

ENDURE AND PERSIST; this pain will turn to your good. —Ovid

DON'T LET THE bastards grind you down.
—Motto of General Joseph W. Stilwell
(his own translation of *illegitimati non carborundum*)

ENJOY WHEN YOU can, and endure when you must. —Goethe

HE THAT CAN'T endure the bad, will not live to see the good.—Jewish proverb

ENDURE, AND SAVE yourself for happier times. —Virgil

Enemies

Ye have heard that it hath been said,
Thou shalt love thy neighbor, and hate thine enemy.
But I say unto you, Love your enemies . . .

—Jesus of Nazareth

INSTEAD OF LOVING your enemies, treat your friends a little better.

—Edgar Watson Howe

INFLICT NOT ON an enemy every injury in your power, for he may afterwards become your friend. . . .

O WISE MAN, wash your hands of that friend who associates with your enemies.

—Saadi

TREAT YOUR FRIEND as if he might become an enemy.   —Publilius Syrus

OBSERVE YOUR ENEMIES, for they first find out your faults.   —Antisthenes

USE YOUR ENEMY'S hand to catch a snake.   —Persian proverb

BE THINE ENEMY an ant, see in him an elephant.   —Turkish proverb

Energy

BE MASTER OF your petty annoyances and conserve your energies for the big, worthwhile things. It isn't the mountain ahead that wears you out—it's the grain of sand in your shoe. —Robert Service

[DON'T] SPEND TEN dollars' worth of energy on a ten-cent problem. . . . There are millions of want-to's and have-to's in life. Ultimately, these pressures create stress only when your time and energy-spending decisions aren't consistent with your goals, beliefs and values. —Dr. Donald A. Tubesing

BE SURE TO get enough sleep and rest, since fatigue can reduce your ability to cope with stress. Eat regular, well-balanced meals with enough variety to assure good nutrition and enough complex carbohydrates (starchy foods) to guarantee a ready energy reserve. Reverse the typical American meal pattern and instead eat like a king for breakfast, a prince for lunch, and a pauper for supper. . . . Revitalize through exercise. . . . Exercise enhances, rather than saps, your energy; it also has a distinct relaxing effect. —Jane E. Brody

WE MUST HAVE ENERGY. —Garp

THE WAY YOU define yourself as a writer is that you write every time you have a free minute. If you didn't behave that way you would never do anything. —John Irving

Enjoyment

ENJOY YOURSELF—IT'S later than you think. —Chinese proverb

ENJOY PRESENT PLEASURES in such a way as not to injure future ones.—Seneca

[DON'T WAIT] FOR the day when "you can relax" or when "your problems will be over." The struggles of life never end. Most good things in life are fleeting and transitory. Enjoy them. Don't waste time looking forward to the "happy ending" to all your troubles.—Drs. Robert L. Woolfold and Frank C. Richardson

MY ADVICE TO you is not to inquire why or whither, but just enjoy your ice cream while it's on your plate—that's my philosophy. —Thornton Wilder

Enterprise

MAKE THE BEST use of what is in your power, and take the rest as it happens. —Epictetus

BEFORE UNDERTAKING ANY design, weigh the glory of the action with the danger of the attempt. If the glory outweigh the danger it is cowardice to neglect it; if the danger exceed the glory, it is rashness to attempt it; if the balances stand poised, let thine own genius cast them. —Francis Quarles

ATTEMPT THE END, and never stand to doubt; nothing so hard but search will find it out. —Robert Herrick

DON'T BE AFRAID of opposition. Remember, a kite rises against, not with the wind. —Hamilton Wright Mabie

WHAT PEOPLE SAY you cannot do, you try and find that you can. —Henry David Thoreau

BE A PIANIST, not a piano. —A. R. Orage

Enthusiasm

WORK PERSEVERINGLY; WORK can be made into a pleasure, and alone is profitable to man, to his city, to his country. Your language has borrowed from ours the beautiful word enthusiasm, bequeathed to us by the Greeks: *ev veos,* "an inward God."

—Louis Pasteur

THROW YOUR HEART over the fence and the rest will follow.

—Norman Vincent Peale

LET US RECOGNIZE the beauty of true enthusiasm; and whatever we may do to enlighten ourselves or others, guard against checking or chilling a single earnest sentiment.

—Henry T. Tuckerman

IF YOU AREN'T fired with enthusiasm, you will be fired with enthusiasm.

—Vince Lombardi

Envy/Jealousy

O, beware, my lord, of jealousy!
It is the green-ey'd monster which doth mock
The meat it feeds on.

—Iago, in Shakespeare's
Othello the Moor of Venice

IT IS ENOUGH if you don't freeze in the cold and thirst and hunger don't claw at your sides. If your back isn't broken, if your feet can walk, if both arms can bend, if both eyes can see, and if both ears hear, then whom should you envy? And why? Our envy of others devours us most of all. Rub your eyes and purify your heart and prize above all else in the world those who love you and who wish you well. Do not hurt or scold them, and never part from any of them in anger. After all, you simply do not know; it might be your last act.

—Alexander Solzhenitsyn

Error

LOVE TRUTH, AND pardon error. —Voltaire

MY PRINCIPAL METHOD for defeating error and heresy is, by establishing the truth. One purposes to fill a bushel with tares; but if I can fill it first with wheat, I may defy his attempts. —John Newton

WHEN THE MOST insignificant person tells us we are in error, we should listen, and examine ourselves, and see if it is so. To believe it possible we may be in error, is the first step toward getting out of it. —Johann K. Lavater

GIVE ME A good fruitful error any time, full of seeds, bursting with its own corrections. You can keep your sterile truth for yourself. —Vilfredo Pareto

Ethics

YOU ARE NOT to do evil that good may come of it. —Legal maxim

PREFER LOSS TO the wealth of dishonest gain; the former vexes you for a time; the latter will bring you lasting remorse. —Chilo

> O ye who lead,
> Take heed!
> Blindness we may forgive, but baseness we will smite.
> —William Vaughn Moody

IF YOU KNOW that a thing is unrighteous, then use all dispatch in putting an end to it—why wait till next year? —Mencius

REMEMBER THE END, and thou shalt never do amiss.—Ecclesiasticus, Apochrypha

HERE'S MY GOLDEN RULE for a tarnished age: Be fair with others, but then keep after them until they're fair with you. —Alan Alda

Evil

SET GOOD AGAINST evil. —English proverb

WE SOMETIMES LEARN more from the sight of evil than from an example of good; and it is well to accustom ourselves to profit by the evil which is so common, while that which is good is so rare. —Blaise Pascal

For every evil under the sun,
  There is a remedy or there is none.
If there be one, try and find it,
  If there be none, never mind it.

—Old English rhyme

BE NOT OVERCOME of evil, but overcome evil with good.

—Epistle of Paul the Apostle
to the Romans, New Testament

NEVER OPEN THE door to a lesser evil, for other and greater ones invariably slink in after it. —Baltasar Gracian

OF TWO EVILS, choose the least. —Erasmus

DON'T LET US make imaginary evils, when you know we have so many real ones to encounter. —Oliver Goldsmith

EVERY MINUTE YOU are thinking of evil, you might have been thinking of good instead. Refuse to pander to a morbid interest in your own misdeeds. Pick yourself up, be sorry, shake yourself, and go on again. —Evelyn Underhill

KEEP FIVE YARDS from a carriage, ten yards from a horse, and a hundred yards from an elephant; but the distance one should keep from a wicked man cannot be measured. —Indian proverb

ACCUSTOM YOURSELF TO submit on every occasion to a small present evil, to obtain a greater distant good. This will give decision, tone and energy to the mind, which, thus disciplined, will often reap victory from defeat and honor from repulse. —Charles Caleb Colton

Example

Be stirring as the time; be fire with fire;
Threaten the threat'ner, and outface the brow
Of bragging horror: so shall inferior eyes
That borrow their behaviors from the great;
Grow great by your example, and put on
The dauntless spirit of resolution.

—Bastard, in Shakespeare's
The Life and Death of King John

SO ACT THAT your principle of action might safely be made a law for the whole world.

—Immanuel Kant

IF YOU WOULD convince a man that he does wrong, do right. Men will believe what they see.

—Henry David Thoreau

YOU CAN PREACH a better sermon with your life than with your lips.

—Oliver Goldsmith

ALWAYS DO RIGHT. This will surprise some people and astonish the rest.

—Mark Twain

Excellence

AIM AT PERFECTION in everything, though in most things it is unattainable; however, they who aim at it, and persevere, will come much nearer to it than those whose laziness and despondency make them give it up as unattainable.

—Lord Chesterfield

TO GET THE best out of a man go to what is best in him.　　—Daniel Considine

IF I HAD given you any parting advice it would I think all have been comprised in this one sentence: to live up always to the best and highest you know.

　　　　　　　　　　　　　　　　　　　　—Hannah Whitall Smith

HIT THE BALL over the fence and you can take your time going around the bases.　　　　　　　　　　　　　　　　　　　　—John W. Raper

Excess

GNOTHI SEAUTON. (KNOW THYSELF.)
Meden agan. (Nothing in excess.)　　　　　—Engraved by the Seven Wise Men,
　　　　　　　　　　　　　　　　　　Temple of Apollo at Delphi

USE, DO NOT abuse; neither abstinence nor excess ever renders man happy.
　　　　　　　　　　　　　　　　　　　　　　　—Voltaire

　　　　　　Avoid extremes; and shun the fault of such
　　　　　　Who still are pleas'd too little or too much.

　　　　　　　　　　　　　　　　　　　　—Alexander Pope

REFRAIN TONIGHT, AND that shall lend a hand of easiness to the next absti-nence; the next more easy; for use can almost change the stamp of nature, and either curb the devil or throw him out with wondrous potency.

　　　　　　　　　　　　　　　　　—Hamlet, in Shakespeare's
　　　　　　　　　　　　　　　　　Hamlet Prince of Denmark

Expectation

IF YOU EXPECT perfection from people, your whole life is a series of disappointments, grumblings and complaints. If, on the contrary, you pitch your expectations low, taking folks as the inefficient creatures which they are, you are frequently surprised by having them perform better than you had hoped.

—Bruce Barton

BEFORE WE SET our hearts too much upon anything, let us examine how happy those are who already possess it. —François de La Rochefoucauld

DO NOT ANTICIPATE trouble, or worry about what may never happen. Keep in the sunlight. —Benjamin Franklin

Lighten griefs with hopes of a brighter morrow
Temper joy, in fear of a change of fortune.

—Horace

DON'T FALL BEFORE you're pushed. —English proverb

Experience

THE MAIN POINT is getting some experience. . . . Think how it is in that tennis game or in that race or whatever it is. When the whistle blows you have only a limited amount of time to do what you have to do. You either do it then or you don't do it at all. —Justice Byron White

YOU CANNOT ACQUIRE experience by making experiments. You cannot create experience. You must undergo it. —Albert Camus

WE SHOULD BE careful to get out of an experience only the wisdom that is in it —and stop there; lest we be like the cat that sits down on a hot stove-lid. She will never sit down on a hot stove-lid again—and that is well; but also she will never sit down on a cold one anymore. —Mark Twain

> Nor deem the irrevocable past
> As wholly wasted, wholly vain
> If, rising on its wrecks, at last
> To something nobler we attain.
> —Henry Wadsworth Longfellow

TO KNOW THE road ahead, ask those coming back. —Chinese proverb

Experimentation

IT IS COMMON sense to take a method and try it. If it fails, admit it frankly and try another. But above all, try something. —Franklin D. Roosevelt

PROVE ALL THINGS; hold fast that which is good. —I Thessalonians

DON'T BE TOO timid and squeamish about your actions. All life is an experiment. The more experiments you make the better. —Ralph Waldo Emerson

RAISE YOUR SAIL one foot and you get ten feet of wind. —Chinese proverb

Exploration

Forward, forward let us range,
Let the great world spin for ever down the ringing
grooves of change.

—Alfred, Lord Tennyson

LET BOTH SIDES seek to invoke the wonders of science instead of its terrors. Together let us explore the stars, conquer the deserts, eradicate disease, tap the ocean depths and encourage the arts and commerce. —John F. Kennedy

EVERYTHING IN SPACE obeys the laws of physics. If you know these laws, and obey them, space will treat you kindly. And don't tell me man doesn't belong out there. Man belongs wherever he wants to go—and he'll do plenty well when he gets there. —Wernher von Braun

Facetious Advice

SMACK YOUR CHILD every day. If you don't know why—he does.—Joey Adams

NEVER LEARN TO do anything: If you don't learn, you'll always find someone else who'll do it for you.
—Mark Twain

WHEN LYING, BE emphatic and indignant, thus behaving like your children.
—William Feather

DON'T JUST STAND there—do something.
—Anonymous

DON'T JUST DO something—stand there.—George Shultz (on government meddling)

DON'T JUST STAND there—undo something.
—Murray Weidenbaum (on government regulation)

NEVER EAT ANYTHING at one sitting that you can't lift.
—Miss Piggy, puppet character

IF YOU WANT to recapture your youth, just cut off his allowance.—Al Bernstein

NEVER LEND A book, for no one ever returns them; the only books I have in my library are books that other folks have lent me.
—Anatole France

IF YOUR WIFE wants to learn to drive, don't stand in her way. —Sam Levenson

IT IS BETTER to have loafed and lost than never to have loafed at all.
—James Thurber

LAUGH AND THE world laughs with you; snore and you sleep alone.
—Anthony Burgess

BUY OLD MASTERS. They fetch a much better price than old mistresses.
—Lord Beaverbrook

IF THREE PEOPLE say you are an ass, put on a bridle. —Spanish proverb

NEVER GET MARRIED in the morning, 'cause you may never know who you'll meet that night. —Paul Hornung

IF YOU'RE GOING to do something tonight that you'll be sorry for tomorrow morning, sleep late. —Henny Youngman

YOU CAN GET a lot more done with a kind word and a gun, than with a kind word alone. —Gangster Al Capone,
quoted jocularly by economist Walter Heller,
in connection with wage and price controls

IN REVILING, IT is not necessary to prepare a preliminary draft.
—Chinese proverb

NO PROBLEM IS so big or so complicated that it can't be run away from.
—Linus, *Peanuts* cartoon character

DO NOT JOIN encounter groups. If you enjoy being made to feel inadequate, call your mother. —Liz Smith

GET THE FACTS first. You can distort them later. —Mark Twain

VISIT, THAT YE be not visited. —Don Herold

WE OUGHT NEVER to do wrong when people are looking. —Mark Twain

THE ONLY WAY to keep your health is to eat what you don't want, drink what you don't like and do what you'd rather not. —Mark Twain

> Stick close to your desks and never go to sea,
> And you'll be the ruler of the Queen's Navee.
>
> —W. S. Gilbert

NEVER MAKE FORECASTS, especially about the future. —Samuel Goldwyn

NEVER GO TO a doctor whose office plants have died. —Erma Bombeck

THERE ARE THREE ways to get something done; do it yourself, hire someone, or forbid your kids to do it. —Monta Crane

DON'T ASK THE barber whether you need a haircut. —Daniel Greenberg

PANIC INSTRUCTION FOR INDUSTRIAL ENGINEERS: When you don't know what to do, walk fast and look worried. —Paul Dickson

THE MOST IMPORTANT thing in acting is honesty. Once you've learned to fake that, you're in. —Attributed to Samuel Goldwyn by Donald Sutherland

ALWAYS CARRY A flagon of whisky in case of snakebite and furthermore always carry a small snake.
—W. C. Fields

DO NOT EXAGGERATE: 1) when performing neurosurgery; 2) in writing military dispatches (before the battle); 3) on job applications (if you are clumsy and may get caught); 4) when running the Bureau of the Budget; 5) in marriage.

EXAGGERATION MAY BE HELPFUL: 1) in lovemaking and courtship; 2) in leading a cavalry charge; 3) when speaking at funerals; 4) when defending a murderer; 5) in military dispatches (after the battle); 6) in political speeches; 7) when writing thank-you notes.
—Lance Morrow

(*See also* Bad Advice, Counsel, Questionable Advice, and Fatherly Advice.)

Facts

APPROACH EACH NEW problem not with a view of finding what you hope will be there, but to get the truth, the realities that must be grappled with. You may not like what you find. In that case you are entitled to try to change it. But do not deceive yourself as to what you do find to be the facts of the situation.
—Bernard M. Baruch

SIT DOWN BEFORE fact as a little child, be prepared to give up every preconceived notion, follow humbly wherever and whatever abysses nature leads, or you will learn nothing.

GOD GIVE ME strength to face a fact though it slay me.
—Thomas H. Huxley

ACCUSTOM YOURSELF TO the roughest and simplest scientific tools. Perfect as the wing of a bird may be, it will never enable the bird to fly if unsupported by the air. Facts are the air of science. Without them a man of science can never rise. Without them your theories are vain surmises. But while you are studying, observing, experimenting, do not remain content with the surface of things. Do not become a mere recorder of facts, but try to penetrate the mystery of their origin. Seek obstinately for the laws that govern them. —Ivan Pavlov

Family

LOOK FOR THE good, not the evil, in the conduct of members of the family.
—Jewish proverb

IF YOU CANNOT get rid of the family skeleton, you may as well make it dance.
—George Bernard Shaw

VISIT YOUR AUNT, but not every day; and call at your brother's, but not every night.
—Benjamin Franklin

NO MATTER HOW much you disagree with your kin, if you are a thoroughbred you will not discuss their shortcomings with the neighbors. —Tom Thompson

DISCIPLINE YOUR FAMILY to the simple needs of life. Hence the Torah teaches a rule of conduct—that a person should not accustom his son to meat and wine.
—Babylonian Talmud, tractate Hullin

Fatherly Advice

BE YOU, MY dear, the link of love, union and peace for the whole family. The world will give you the more credit for it, in proportion to the difficulty of the task.
—Thomas Jefferson,
advice to his daughter, Martha

DEAR PIE:

Things to worry about:

Worry about courage.
Worry about cleanliness.
Worry about efficiency. . . .

Things not to worry about:

Don't worry about popular opinion.
Don't worry about dolls.
Don't worry about the past.
Don't worry about the future.
Don't worry about growing up.
Don't worry about anybody getting ahead of you.
Don't worry about triumph.
Don't worry about failure unless it comes through your own fault. . . .
Don't worry about parents.
Don't worry about boys.
Don't worry about disappointments.
Don't worry about pleasures.
Don't worry about satisfactions.

Things to think about:

What am I really aiming at?
How good am I really in comparison to my contemporaries in regard to:
(a) Scholarship

(b) Do I really understand about people and am I able to get along with them?
(c) Am I trying to make my body a useful instrument or am I neglecting it?
With dearest love,

—F. Scott Fitzgerald,
from a letter to his daughter, Frances, 1933

(*See also* Bad Advice, Counsel, Facetious Advice, and Questionable Advice.)

Faults

IF THE LADY has anything difficult in her disposition, avoid what is rough, and attach her good qualities to you. Consider what are otherwise as a bad stop on your harpsichord. Do not touch on it, but make yourself happy with the good ones. Every human being, my dear, must be viewed according to what it is good for, for none of us, no, not one, is perfect; and were we to love none who had imperfections, this would be a desert for our love. All we can do is to make the best of our friends; love and cherish what is good in them, and keep out of the way of what is bad: but no more think of rejecting them for it than of throwing away a piece of music for a flat passage or two. —Thomas Jefferson

Be to her virtues very kind.
Be to her faults a little blind.

—Matthew Prior

ENDEAVOR TO BE always patient of the faults and imperfections of others for thou hast many faults and imperfections of thine own that require forbearance. If thou are not able to make thyself that which thou wishest, how canst thou expect to mold another in conformity to thy will? —Thomas à Kempis

AN INFATUATED YOUNG man sought counsel at the bazaar of an ancient and prayed the ancient to tell him how he might learn of his fair lady's faults. "Go forth among her women friends," spake the venerable one, "and praise her in their hearing."
—George Jean Nathan

CONCEAL A FLAW, and the world will imagine the worst.
—Martial

> Press not a falling man too far; 'tis virtue:
> His faults lie open to the laws; let them,
> Not you, correct him.
>
> —Lord Chamberlain, in Shakespeare's
> *The Life of King Henry VIII*

THINK NOT THOSE faithful who praise all thy words and actions; but those who kindly reprove thy faults.
—Socrates

LOOK FOR THE good things, not the faults. It takes a good deal bigger-sized brain to find out what is not wrong with people and things, than to find out what is wrong.
—R. L. Sharpe

Fear

THE FIRST DUTY of man is that of subduing fear. We must get rid of fear; we cannot act at all till then. A man's acts are slavish, not true but specious; his very thoughts are false, he thinks too as a slave and coward, till he have got fear under his feet.
—Thomas Carlyle

SO LET ME assert my firm belief that the only thing we have to fear is fear itself —nameless, unreasoning, unjustified terror which paralyzes needed efforts to convert retreat into advance.
—Franklin D. Roosevelt

YOU GAIN STRENGTH, courage and confidence by every experience in which you really stop to look fear in the face. You are able to say to yourself, "I have lived through this horror. I can take the next thing that comes along." You must do the thing you think you cannot do. —Eleanor Roosevelt

THE FIRST AND great commandment is: Don't let them scare you.—Elmer Davis

A THOUSAND FEARFUL images and dire suggestions glance along the mind when it is moody and discontented with itself. Command them to stand and show themselves, and you presently assert the power of reason over imagination. —Sir Walter Scott

LET THE FEAR of danger be a spur to prevent it; he that fears not, gives advantage to the danger. —Francis Quarles

KEEP YOUR FEARS to yourself, but share your courage with others.

—Robert Louis Stevenson

IF YOU ARE a terror to many, then beware of many. —Ausonius

THERE ARE MOMENTS when everything goes well; don't be frightened, it won't last. —Jules Renard

Feelings

FORMULATE YOUR FEELINGS as well as your thoughts. —A. R. Orage

DO NOT VIOLENCE to yourself; respect in yourself the oscillations of feeling: they are your life and your nature; a wiser than you made them.—Henri F. Amiel

NEVER APOLOGIZE FOR showing feeling. When you do so, you apologize for truth. —Benjamin Disraeli

LOVE GOD AND trust your feelings. Be loyal to them. Don't betray them.

—Robert C. Pollock

WHERE THE HEART lies, let the brain lie also. —Robert Browning

Forbearance

IF THOU WOULD'ST be borne with, then bear with others. —Thomas Fuller

CULTIVATE FORBEARANCE TILL your heart yields a fine crop of it. Pray for a short memory as to all unkindnesses. —Charles Haddon Spurgeon

DESPISE NOT ANY man, and do not spurn anything; for there is no man who has not his hour, nor is there anything that has not its place. —Ben Azai, Mishna

Teach me to feel another's woe,
To hide the fault I see;
That mercy I to others show,
That mercy show to me.

—Alexander Pope

(*See also* Patience.)

Forgiveness

FORGIVE MANY THINGS in others; nothing in yourself. —Ausonius

ALWAYS FORGIVE YOUR enemies; nothing annoys them so much.—Oscar Wilde

The truest joys they seldom prove,
Who free from quarrels live;
'Tis the most tender part of love,
Each other to forgive.

—John Sheffield

DON'T TELL YOUR friends their social faults; they will cure the fault and never forgive you. —Logan Pearsall Smith

Fortune

ACCEPT THE THINGS to which fate binds you. And love the people with whom fate brings you together, but do so with all your heart. —Marcus Aurelius

DEPEND NOT ON fortune, but on conduct. —Publilius Syrus

WE SHOULD MANAGE our fortunes as we do our health—enjoy it when good, be patient when it is bad, and never apply violent remedies except in an extreme necessity. —François de La Rochefoucauld

WORK AND ACQUIRE, and thou hast chained the wheel of Chance. —Ralph Waldo Emerson

Freedom of the Press

LET IT BE impressed upon your minds, let it be instilled into your children, that the liberty of the press is the palladium of all the civil, political, and religious rights. —Junius

UNLESS WARINESS BE used, as good almost kill a man as kill a good book . . . he who destroys a good book, kills reason itself, kills the image of God, as it were, in the eye. Many a man lives a burden to the earth; but a good book is the precious lifeblood of a masterspirit. . . . We should be wary, therefore, what persecution we raise against the living labours of public men, how we spill that seasoned life of man, preserved and stored up in books . . . whereof the execution ends not in the slaying of an elemental life, but strikes at the ethereal and fifth essence, the breath of reason itself; slays an immortality rather than a life. —John Milton

BE NOT INTIMIDATED . . . by any terrors, from publishing with the utmost freedom whatever can be warranted by the laws of your country; nor suffer yourselves to be wheedled out of your liberty by any pretenses of politeness, delicacy or decency. These, as they are often used, are but three different names for hypocrisy, chicanery, and cowardice. —John Adams

DON'T JOIN THE book burners. Don't think you're going to conceal faults by concealing evidence that they never existed. Don't be afraid to go in your library and read every book. . . . —Dwight D. Eisenhower

LET CHILDREN READ whatever they want and then talk about it with them. If parents and kids can talk together, we won't have as much censorship because we won't have as much fear. —Judy Blume

Friendship

Those friends thou hast, and their adoption tried,
Grapple them to thy soul with hoops of steel.
But do not dull thy palm with entertainment
Of each new hatched, unfledged comrade.

—Polonius, in Shakespeare's
Hamlet Prince of Denmark

BE COURTEOUS TO all, but intimate with few, and let those few be well tried before you give them your confidence. True friendship is a plant of slow growth, and must undergo and withstand the shocks of adversity before it is entitled to the appellation. —George Washington

IF A MAN does not make new acquaintances as he advances through life, he will soon find himself alone. A man should keep his friendships in constant repair.
—Samuel Johnson

BE MORE PROMPT to go to a friend in adversity than in prosperity. —Chilo

NEVER REFUSE ANY advance of friendship, for if nine out of ten bring you nothing, one alone may repay you.
—Madame de Tencin

WHEN A FRIEND is in trouble, don't annoy him by asking if there is any thing you can do. Think up something appropriate and do it. —E. W. Howe

IF IT'S VERY painful for you to criticize your friends—you're safe in doing it. But if you take the slightest pleasure in it—that's the time to hold your tongue.
—Alice Duer Miller

THE ONLY WAY to have a friend is to be one. —Ralph Waldo Emerson

GO OFTEN TO the house of thy friend; for weeds soon choke up the unused path.
—Scandinavian proverb

DO NOT PROTECT yourself by a fence, but rather by your friends.—Czech proverb

DON'T LEAD ME; I may not follow. Don't walk behind me; I may not lead. Walk beside me and be my friend. —Anonymous line quoted by Jacqueline Bisset

Future

ABRIDGE YOUR HOPES in proportion to the shortness of the span of human life, for while we converse, the hours, as if envious of our pleasure, fly away; enjoy therefore the present time, and trust not too much to what tomorrow may produce.
—Horace

YOU BETTER LIVE your best and act your best and think your best today, for today is the sure preparation for tomorrow and all the other tomorrows that follow.
—Harriet Martineau

IT IS A mistake to try to look too far ahead. The chain of destiny can only be grasped one link at a time.
—Sir Winston Churchill

NONE OF US knows what is ahead. . . . The important thing is to use today wisely and well, and face tomorrow eagerly and cheerfully and with the certainty that we shall be equal to what it brings.
—Channing Pollock

LIGHT TOMORROW WITH to-day!
—Elizabeth Barrett Browning

GAMBLING · GENEROSITY · GIFTS/GIVING · GOALS/OBJECTIVES · GOD · GOLDEN RULE

GOOD HUMOR · GOODNESS · GOSSIP · GOVERNMENT · GRATITUDE · GREATNESS · GRIEF

Gambling

PLAY NOT FOR gain, but sport; who plays for more than he can lose with pleasure stakes his heart.
—George Herbert

TRUE LUCK CONSISTS not in holding the best of the cards at the table: Luckiest is he who knows just when to rise and go home.
—John Hay

IT MAY BE that the race is not always to the swift, nor the battle to the strong—but that's the way to bet.
—Damon Runyon

MILLIONS OF WORDS are written annually purporting to tell how to beat the races, whereas the best possible advice on the subject is found in the three monosyllables: "Do not try."
—Dan Parker

Generosity

DO IT NOW. It is not safe to leave a generous feeling to the cooling influences of the world.
—Thomas Guthrie

HE WHO CONFERS a favor should at once forget it, if he is not to show a sordid ungenerous spirit. To remind a man of a kindness conferred and to talk of it, is little different from reproach.
—Demosthenes

He who would do good to another must
do it in minute particulars:
General good is the plea of the scoun-
drel, hypocrite and flatterer.

For art and science cannot exist but in
minutely organized particulars.

—William Blake

BE CHARITABLE BEFORE wealth makes thee covetous.   —Sir Thomas Browne

WHEN YOU HAVE given nothing, ask for nothing.   —Albanian proverb

Gifts/Giving

THE GREAT ART of giving consists in this: the gift should cost very little and yet
be greatly coveted, so that it may be the more highly appreciated.

—Baltasar Gracian

WHEN THOU MAKEST presents, let them be of such things as will last long; to
the end they may be in some sort immortal, and may frequently refresh the
memory of the receiver.   —Thomas Fuller

Win her with gifts, if she respect not words;
Dumb jewels often, in their silent kind,
More quick than words, do move a woman's mind.

—Valentine, in Shakespeare's
Two Gentlemen of Verona

NOR DO I bid you give your mistress costly gifts; let them be small, but choose
your small gifts cunningly and well.   —Ovid

IN CHOOSING PRESENTS people should remember that the whole point of a
present is that it is an extra.   —E. V. Lucas

YOU MAY SEND poetry to the rich; to poor men give substantial presents.

—Martial

BEFORE GIVING, LET us try to acquire; for this last is a duty wherefrom we are not relieved by the fact of our giving. —Maurice Maeterlinck

HE WHO RECEIVES a benefit should never forget it; he who bestows should never remember it. —Pierre Charron

WHEN YOU GIVE, take to yourself no credit for generosity, unless you deny yourself something in order that you may give. —Sir Henry Taylor

PURCHASE NOT FRIENDS by gifts; when thou ceasest to give, such will cease to love. —Thomas Fuller

TO RECEIVE A present handsomely and in a right spirit, even when you have none to give in return, is to give one in return. —Leigh Hunt

> Give all thou canst; high Heaven rejects the lore
> Of nicely-calculated less or more.

—William Wordsworth

WE MUST NOT only give what we *have;* we must also give what we *are.*

—Désiré Joseph Cardinal Mercier

WE MUST NOT be unjust and exact from ourselves what it is not in our power to give. —Saint Francis de Sales

THE BEST THING to give to your enemy is forgiveness; to an opponent, tolerance; to a friend, your heart; to your child, a good example; to a father, deference; to your mother, conduct that will make her proud of you; to yourself, respect; to all men, charity. —Francis Maitland Balfour

GET NOT YOUR friends by bare compliments, but by giving them sensible tokens of your love.
—Socrates

Goals/Objectives

WE NEED OBJECTIVES. We need focus and direction. Most of all, we need the sense of accomplishment that comes from achieving what we set out to do . . . it's important to make plans, even if we decide to change them, so that at least for the moment we know where we're going and we can have a sense of progress. In the long run, it's frustrating, not liberating, to be like the airplane pilot who radios, "I have good news and bad news. The good news is that I'm making excellent time. The bad news is that I'm lost!" Or, putting it another way, a sailor without a destination cannot hope for a favorable wind.—Leon Tec, M.D.

IT'S NOT ENOUGH to be busy . . . the question is: What are we busy about?
—Henry David Thoreau

THE PERSON WHO makes a success of living is the one who sees his goal steadily and aims for it unswervingly. That is dedication.   —Cecil B. De Mille

THE MOST IMPORTANT thing is to have a code of life, to know how to live. Find yourself a port of destination—and practice what I call altruistic egoism. . . . If you are desired, if you are necessary, then you are safe.—Dr. Hans Selye

God

Know first, the heaven, the earth, the main,
The moon's pale orb, the starry train,
Are nourished by a soul,

A bright intelligence, whose flame
Glows in each member of the frame,
And stirs the mighty whole.

—Virgil

LIVE WITH MEN as if God saw you, and talk to God as if men were listening.

—Athenodorus

WE CANNOT TOO often think, that there is a never sleeping eye that reads the heart, and registers our thoughts.

—Francis Bacon

FEAR GOD, YES, but don't be afraid of Him.

—J. A. Spender

LIVE NEAR TO God, and so all things will appear to you little in comparison with eternal realities.

—R. M. McCheyne

HE WHO DESIRES to see the living God face to face should not seek Him in the empty firmament of his mind, but in human love.

—Feodor Dostoevsky

LOOK UP, LAUGH, love and live. In my lifetime I've done that. I do look up and communicate lovingly with my friend up there . . . although I know God is within. I look up and laugh and live.

—Mary Martin

Golden Rule

ALL THINGS WHATSOEVER ye would that men should do to you, do ye even so to them: for this is the Law and the Prophets.

—Jesus of Nazareth

WHAT IS HATEFUL to you, do not to your fellowman. That is the entire Law; all the rest is commentary.

—The Talmud

TSZE-KUNG ASKED, "Is there one word which may serve as a rule of practice for all of one's life?" The Master said, "Is not reciprocity such a word? What you do not want done to yourself, do not do to others." Tsze-loo then said, "I should like, sir, to hear your wishes." The Master said: "In regard to the aged, to give them rest; in regard to friends, to show them sincerity; in regard to the young, to treat them tenderly."

—Confucius, *Analects*

HURT NOT OTHERS in ways that you yourself would find hurtful.

—Udana-Varga (Buddhism)

NO ONE OF you is a believer until he desires for his brother that which he desires for himself.

—Sunnah (Islam)

THIS IS THE sum of duty: Do naught unto others which would cause you pain if done to you.

—Mahabharata (Brahmanism)

WE HAVE COMMITTED the Golden Rule to memory; let us now commit it to life.

—Edwin Markham

Good Humor

WE ARE ALL here for a spell; get all the good laughs you can.　　—Will Rogers

LIVE MERRILY AS thou canst, for by honest mirth we cure many passions of the mind.

—Robert Burton

ALWAYS LAUGH WHEN you can. It is cheap medicine.　　—Lord Byron

> Laugh and the world laughs with you;
> Weep and you weep alone.

—Ella Wheeler Wilcox

LET US MAKE one point . . . that we meet each other with a smile, when it is difficult to smile. . . . Smile at each other, make time for each other in your family.
—Mother Teresa, in her Nobel lecture

Goodness

LIVE NOT AS if you had ten thousand years before you. Necessity is upon you. While you live, while you may, become good.
—Marcus Aurelius

> Be good, sweet maid, and let who will be clever;
> Do noble things, not dream them all day long;
> And so make life, death, and that vast forever
> One grand, sweet song.
>
> —Charles Kingsley

A MAN, TO be greatly good, must imagine intensely and comprehensively; he must put himself in the place of another and in many others; the pains and pleasures of his species must become his own.
—Percy Bysshe Shelley

A MAN, AFTER he has brushed off the dust and chips of his life, will have left only the hard, clean question: Was it good or was it evil? Have I done well—or ill?
—John Steinbeck

> Content thyself to be obscurely good.
> When vice prevails and impious men bear sway,
> The post of honor is a private station.
>
> —Joseph Addison

NO LONGER TALK at all about the kind of man that a good man ought to be, but be such.
—Marcus Aurelius

Gossip

WHAT YOU DON'T see with your eyes, don't invent with your mouth.

—Jewish proverb

WE CANNOT CONTROL the evil tongues of others; but a good life enables us to disregard them.

—Cato the Elder

IF YOU WANT to get the most out of life why the thing to do is to be a gossiper by day and a gossipee by night.

—Ogden Nash

WHOEVER GOSSIPS TO you will gossip about you.

—Spanish proverb

COUNT NOT HIM among your friends who will retail your privacies to the world.

—Publilius Syrus

Government

IF FREEDOM HAD been the happy, simple, relaxed state of ordinary humanity, man would have everywhere been free—whereas through most of time and space he has been in chains. Do not let us make any mistake about this. The natural government of man is servitude. Tyranny is the normal pattern of government.

—Adlai E. Stevenson

IF YOU WANT to understand democracy, spend less time in the library with Plato, and more time in the buses with people.

—Simeon Strunsky

GOVERN A GREAT nation as you would cook a small fish; do not overdo it.

—Lao-tsze

Gratitude

WHEN YOU DRINK the water, remember the spring.

—Chinese proverb

IF WE USE no ceremony toward others, we shall be treated without any. People are soon tired of paying trifling attentions to those who receive them with coldness, and return them with neglect.

—William Hazlitt

THE BEST WAY to be thankful is to use the goods the gods provide you.

—Anthony Trollope

BE THANKFUL F'R what ye have not, Hinnissey—'tis th' on'y safe rule.

—Finley Peter Dunne

PRAISE THE BRIDGE that carried you over.

—George Colman, The Younger

Greatness

BE NOT AFRAID of greatness: some men are born great, some achieve greatness and some have greatness thrust upon them. —Malvolio, in Shakespeare's
Twelfth Night

THE SECRET OF greatness is simple: Do better work than any other man in your field—and keep on doing it. —Wilfred A. Peterson

LET HIM BE great, and love shall follow him. —Ralph Waldo Emerson

IF ANY MAN seeks for greatness, let him forget greatness and ask for truth, and he will find both. —Horace Mann

WORSHIP YOUR HEROES from afar; contact withers them. —Madame Necker

Grief

WHILE GRIEF IS fresh, every attempt to divert only irritates. You must wait till it be digested, and then amusement will dissipate the remains of it.
—Samuel Johnson

Count each affliction, whether light or grave,
God's messenger sent down to thee; do thou
With courtesy receive him . . .
Grief should be
Like joy, majestic, equable, sedate;
Confirming, cleansing, raising, making free;

Strong to consume small troubles; to commend
Great thoughts, grave thoughts, thoughts lasting to the end.

—Aubrey de Vere

Now let the weeping cease;
Let no one mourn again.
These things are in the hands of God.

—Sophocles

WHEN MEETING A friend for the first time after there has been a death close to him, it's appropriate to offer condolences. Keep it very brief and simple, just enough to express sorrow that it happened, and then ask a question that will allow the friend to keep his composure. It can be related to the death, but not to his feeling of loss. Ask if he plans to move, or if most of the family were able to attend the funeral, or if he plans to go away for awhile. . . . If you have privacy, and if the death was recent, it's more likely that the person will want to talk of nothing else, will *need* to talk of nothing else. There's a Hebrew proverb about "wearing out" grief—if you bottle it up, you'll never soften it. "Give sorrow words," said Shakespeare. "The grief that does not speak whispers the o'er-fraught heart and bids it break."

—Barbara Walters

NOT ONLY SHOULD we be unashamed of grief, confident that its expression will not permanently hurt us, but we should also possess the wisdom to talk about our loss and through that creative conversation with friends and companions begin to reconstruct the broken fragments of our lives. . . . We should not resist the sympathy and stimulation of social interaction. We should learn not to grow impatient with the slow healing process of time. . . . We should anticipate these stages in our emotional convalescence: unbearable pain, poignant grief, empty days, resistance to consolation, disinterestedness in life, gradually giving way under the healing sunlight of love, friendship, social challenge, to the

new weaving of a pattern of action and the acceptance of the irresistible challenge of life.
                                        —Rabbi Joshua L. Liebman

Grooming

DON'T WAIT TO experiment with makeup styles until that special evening when you're going out. Instead, choose a free time when you can try different shades, techniques and products in a relaxed way. Decide what you like, what looks good on you. Then, when you really want to look your best, you will be prepared. . . . For daytime, makeup must be natural, lighter. Evening makeup can be more artificial and sophisticated, to harmonize with evening clothes and to fit the occasion. . . . No matter what type of makeup you are using, be sure to check yourself in a different type of light after you have applied it. Different lights bring out different tones, and you don't want any surprises.   —Aida Grey

CUT DOWN ON alcohol and cigarettes to avoid wrinkles. Too much liquor dehydrates the skin, and continually pursing the lips while smoking causes aging lines. . . . Keep your chin up! It's not only good for morale but makes shadows and puffs under the eyes look less dark. . . . It's socially acceptable to refresh your lipstick in a restaurant or other public place, but save a complete makeup redo for the rest room. . . . Feeling down in the dumps? Retouching your lipstick will give you an instant lift. Try it and see.   —Sharon Gold

APPLY YOUR MAKEUP for best results ten to fifteen minutes before going out to allow the makeup to settle and look more natural.   —Charles Hall

DON'T WASTE GOOD perfume by putting it behind your ears. There's nothing there but bone, and perfume belongs to a pulse point. . . . Fragrance rises and diffuses. So unless your lover is a giraffe, it's pointless to apply it in high places.
                                        —Henry Calisher

ADVICE ON A BEAUTY REGIME: Soap, lots of fresh water and a good hand lotion—because you can use it on your body, hands and face. I'm serious; cleansing with soap and lots of water, using your hands—I think that's the best.

—Elizabeth Taylor

Growth

BE NOT AFRAID of growing slowly, be afraid only of standing still.

—Chinese proverb

THE GREAT LAW of culture is: Let each become all that he was capable of being; expand, if possible to his full growth; resisting all impediments, casting off all foreign, especially all noxious adhesions; and show himself at length in his own shape and stature, be these what they may.   —Thomas Carlyle

LIVE ACCORDING TO what you are and you will grow. To grow in one direction when we should be growing in another is an altogether bogus growth.

—Hubert Van Zeller

WE MUST NOT stay as we are, doing always what was done last time, or we shall stick in the mud.   —George Bernard Shaw

YOU MUST GROW like a tree, not like a mushroom.   —Janet Erskine Stuart

Habit

CHOOSE THE LIFE that is most useful, and habit will make it the most agreeable.
—Francis Bacon

CULTIVATE ONLY THE habits that you are willing should master you.
—Elbert Hubbard

KEEP YOURSELF ALIVE by throwing day by day fresh currents of thought and emotion into the things you have come to do from habit.—John Lancaster Spalding

WISE LIVING CONSISTS perhaps less in acquiring good habits than in acquiring as few habits as possible.
—Eric Hoffer

WE OWE OUR children a set of good habits; for habit is to be their best friend or their worst enemy, not only during childhood, but through all the years. We shall therefore need to repeat every now and then nature's irrevocable law: that back of every habit lies a series of acts; that ahead of every act lies a habit; that habit is nine tenths of conduct; that conduct is but character in the making; and that character ends in destiny.
—George Herbert Betts

Handicap

IF I COULD give a message to the physically disabled, it would be this: Overcome self-pity by reaching out to others like you and giving them courage and support. Lift others and you lift yourself. Meet each challenge that your handicap brings with faith; don't give up, no matter what. Be as independent and self-reliant as possible. Educate yourself. And lastly, discover your talents and use them!

TO THE FAMILY and friends of the handicapped, I say: Do not expect any less of them than you would of yourself. Don't sell their abilities short. Give them freedom, encouragement and room to grow, and they will surprise you. If they try, and fail, don't be too quick to pick them up. —Virl Osmond

BE WILLING TO have it so. Acceptance of what has happened is the first step to overcoming the consequences of any misfortune. —William James

EACH OF US must find out for himself that his handicaps, his failures, and shortcomings must be conquered or else he must perish. . . . My weakness—my handlessness—my sense of inferiority has turned out to be my greatest strength. It's not what you have lost, but what you have left that counts. . . . I was able to meet the challenge of utter disaster and master it. For me, this was and is the all important fact—that the human soul, beaten down, overwhelmed, faced by complete failure and ruin, can still rise up against unbearable odds and triumph. —Harold Russell

THE FIRST THING you have to do after suffering a stroke is to tell yourself you won't give up, that you don't want to die, or be cared for like a baby the rest of your life. . . . Now I'm healthy and have only a slight limp and some trouble remembering the names of people and places. But I get better every year, and I'm still working. —Patricia Neal

Happiness

SEEK NOT HAPPINESS too greedily, and be not fearful of happiness.—Lao-tsze

My creed is this:

Happiness is the only good.
The place to be happy is here.

The time to be happy is now.
The way to be happy is to make others so.

—Robert Ingersoll

REAL HAPPINESS IS not dependent on external things. The pond is fed from within. The kind of happiness that stays with you is the happiness that springs from inward thoughts and emotions. You must cultivate your mind if you wish to achieve enduring happiness. You must furnish your mind with interesting thoughts and ideas. For an empty mind seeks pleasure as a substitute for happiness.

—Lillian Eichler Watson paraphrasing
William Lyons Phelps

DO NOT WORRY; eat three square meals a day; say your prayers; be courteous to your creditors; keep your digestion good; exercise; go slow and easy. Maybe there are other things your special case requires to make you happy, but my friend, these I reckon will give you a good life.   —Attributed to Abraham Lincoln
(probably apocryphal)

ENJOY YOUR HAPPINESS while you have it, and while you have it do not too closely scrutinize its foundation.

—Joseph Farrell

Be happy while y'er leevin,
For y'er a lang time deid.

—Scottish proverb

MAKE HAPPY THOSE who are near, and those who are far will come.

—Chinese proverb
(Confucianism)

CHERISH ALL YOUR happy moments: they make a fine cushion for old age.

—Christopher Morley

WHILE THE FATES permit, live happily; life speeds on with hurried step, and with winged days the wheel of the headlong year is turned.   —Seneca

REMEMBER THAT HAPPINESS is a way of travel—not a destination.
—Roy M. Goodman

IF WE CANNOT live so as to be happy, let us at least live so as to deserve it.
—Immanuel Hermann Fichte

GET HAPPINESS OUT of your work or you may never know what happiness is.
—Elbert Hubbard

Hatred

ALWAYS REMEMBER OTHERS may hate you but those who hate you don't win unless you hate them. And then you destroy yourself.
—Richard M. Nixon,
in his White House farewell

LET YOUR INTERESTS be as wide as possible, and let your reactions to the things and persons that interest you be as far as possible friendly rather than hostile.   —Bertrand Russell

HATE NO ONE; hate their vices, not themselves.   —J. G. C. Brainard

I WILL TELL you what to hate. Hate hypocrisy; hate cant, hate intolerance, oppression, injustice.   —F. W. Robertson

LET US NOT look back in anger or forward in fear, but around in awareness.
—James Thurber

Health/Exercise

LOOK TO YOUR health, and if you have it, praise God and value it next to a good conscience; for health is the second blessing that we mortals are capable of—a blessing that money can't buy; therefore value it and be thankful for it.

—Izaak Walton

REFUSE TO BE ill. Never tell people you are ill; never own it to yourself. Illness is one of those things which a man should resist on principle.

—Edward George Bulwer-Lytton

10 Golden Rules for Good Health:
1. Have a checkup every year.
2. Be a non-smoker.
3. Drink in moderation.
4. Count each calorie.
5. Watch your cholesterol.
6. Learn nutritional values.
7. Find time for leisure and vacations.
8. Adjust to life's daily pressures.
9. Develop an exercise program.
10. Understand your physical assets and limitations.

—The American Health Foundation

Better to hunt in fields for health unbought
Than fee the doctor for a nauseous draught.
The wise for cure on exercise depend,
God never made his work for man to mend.

—John Dryden, quoted by
cardiologist Paul Dudley White

—AVOID FRIED MEATS which angry up the blood.
—If your stomach disputes you, lie down and pacify it with cool thoughts.
—Keep the juices flowing by jangling around gently as you move.
—Go very light on the vices, such as carrying on in society. The social rumble ain't restful.

—Avoid running at all times.

—Don't look back. Something might be gaining on you.

—Attributed to Satchel Paige

IF YOU WOULD live in health, be old early.

—Spanish proverb

Hedonism

Let us have Wine and Women, Mirth and Laughter
Sermons and soda water the day after.

—Lord Byron

THERE IS PLEASURE in abundance but you will not find it by seeking for it. I know no occupation in life more barren of results than the permanent seeking of pleasure. Pleasure is a by-product of doing something that is worth doing. Therefore, do not seek pleasure as such. Pleasure comes of seeking something else, and comes by the way. The whole point of enjoying recreation is that it is not your permanent occupation. The man who is seeking pleasure as his main occupation in life never has any recreation, because he never can turn to anything else.

—A. Lawrence Lowell

ONE SHOULD BE just as careful in choosing one's pleasures as in avoiding calamities.

—Chinese proverb

DO NOT BITE at the bait of pleasure till you know there is no hook beneath it.

—Thomas Jefferson

HERE'S A RULE I recommend: Never practice two vices at once.

—Tallulah Bankhead

Help

HELP YOURSELF, AND Heaven will help you.
—La Fontaine

AS LONG AS you derive inner help and comfort from anything . . . keep it.
—Mohandas K. Gandhi

THINK NOT THAT a man will so much as lift up his little finger on your behalf, unless he sees his advantage in it.
—Jeremy Bentham

MISTRUST YOUR ZEAL for doing good to others.
—Abbe Huvelin

HELP YOUR LAME dog o'er a stile.
—Jonathan Swift

Honor

LET HONOR BE as strong to us an obligation as necessity is to others.
—Pliny the Elder

When honor comes to you be ready to take it;
But reach not to seize it before it is near.
—John Boyle O'Reilly

YOU CAN NOT believe in honor until you have achieved it. Better keep yourself clean and bright; you are the window through which you must see the world.
—George Bernard Shaw

LEAVE NOT A stain on thine honor.
—Old Testament

BE HONORABLE YOURSELF if you wish to associate with honorable people.

—Welsh proverb

> In points of honor to be try'd
> All passions must be laid aside;
> Ask no advice, but think alone;
> Suppose the question not your own;
> How shall I act? Is not the case;
> But how would Brutus in my place?
> In such a cause would Cato bleed?
> And how would Socrates proceed?

—Jonathan Swift

> Honor and shame from no condition rise
> Act well your part, there all the honor lies.

—Alexander Pope

IF WE FALL on evil days, let us avoid dishonour—for honour is our only gain in death.

—Aeschylus

Hope

> If you are wise,
> You will mingle one thing with
> the other
> not hoping without
> doubt, not doubting
> without hope.

—Seneca

BEFORE YOU GIVE up hope, turn back and read the attacks that were made upon Lincoln.

—Bruce Barton

DO NOT INVEST your whole life in one hope.

—Austin O'Malley

> Say not the struggle naught availeth,
>   The labour and the wounds are vain,
> The enemy faints not, nor faileth
>   And as things have been they remain.
>
> And not by eastern windows only,
>   When daylight comes, comes in the light;
> In front the sun climbs slow, how slowly!
>   But westward, look, the land is bright!

—Arthur Hugh Clough

Hospitality

BE NOT FORGETFUL to entertain strangers; for thereby some have entertained angels unawares.

—Epistle of Paul The Apostle
to the Hebrews, New Testament

> True friendship's laws are by this rule exprest,
> Welcome the coming, speed the parting guest.

IT IS EQUALLY offensive to speed a guest who would like to stay and to detain one who is anxious to leave.

—Homer

WITHDRAW THY FOOT from thy neighbor's house; lest he be weary of thee, and so hate thee.

—Old Testament, Proverbs

IF YOU ARE a host to your guest, be a host to his dog also. —Russian proverb

House/Home

DETERMINE WHAT SORT of a house will be fit for you; determine to work for it, to get it . . . one that you can entirely enjoy and manage, but which you will not be proud of except as you make it charming in its modesty. —John Ruskin

ASK ABOUT YOUR neighbors, then buy the house. —Jewish proverb

STINT YOURSELF, AS you think good, in other things; but don't scruple freedom in brightening home. Gay furniture and a brilliant garden are a sight day by day, and make life blither. —Sir Thomas F. Buxton

HOUSES ARE BUILT to live in, more than to look on; therefore let use be preferred before uniformity, except where both may be had. —Francis Bacon

Be not as a lion in thy house,
Nor frantick among thy servants.

—Apochrypha

BE NOT TOO familiar with thy servants; at first it may beget love, but in the end 'twill breed contempt.

. . . IF THOU HAS a loitering servant, send him on thy errand just before his dinner. —Thomas Fuller

Humanity

YOU MUST NOT lose faith in humanity. Humanity is an ocean; if a few drops of the ocean are dirty, the ocean does not become dirty. —Mohandas K. Gandhi

SO LONG AS we live among men, let us cherish humanity. —Seneca

TAKE UPON YOURSELF as much humanity as possible. —André Gide

WE MUST LEARN to live together as brothers or perish together as fools.
—Dr. Martin Luther King, Jr.

DON'T OVERESTIMATE THE decency of the human race. —H. L. Mencken

Humility

THE TRUE WAY to be humble is not to stoop till you are smaller than yourself, but to stand at your real height against some higher nature that shall show you what the real smallness of your greatest greatness is. —Phillips Brooks

NEVER BE HAUGHTY to the humble; never be humble to the haughty.
—Jefferson Davis

DO NOT PRACTICE excessive humility. —Dr. John Todd

And what doth the Lord require of thee,
But to do justice and to love mercy,
And to walk humbly with thy God.

—Micah, Hebrew prophet

BE HUMBLE, FOR the worst thing in the world is of the same stuff as you; be confident, for the stars are of the same stuff as you.　　　—Nicholai Velimrovie

DON'T BE SO humble. You're not that great.　　　—Golda Meir

IDEALISM · IDEAS · ILLNESS · IMAGINATION · IMMORTALITY · IMPOSSIBILITY

INDIVIDUALITY/ORIGINALITY · INDUSTRY/PRODUCTIVITY · INFLUENCE · INITIATIVE · INSULT

Idealism

YOU MUST BEGIN with an ideal and end with an ideal.—Sir Frederick G. Banting

WE NEED YOU, we need your youth, your strength, and your idealism, to help us make right that which is wrong. I know you have been critically looking at the mores and customs of the past and questioning their value. Every generation does that. But don't discard the time-tested values upon which civilization is built just because they are old. More important, don't let the doom criers and the cynics persuade you that the best is past—that from here it's all downhill. Each generation sees farther than the generation preceding it because it stands on the shoulders of that generation. You will have opportunities beyond anything we've ever known. . . .
—Ronald Reagan,
Speech at the University of Notre Dame
May 17, 1981

IDEALS ARE LIKE stars: you will not succeed in touching them with your hands, but like the seafaring man on the ocean desert of waters, you choose them as your guides, and following them, you reach your destiny. —Carl Schurz

DON'T PART COMPANY with your ideals. They are anchors in a storm.
—Arnold Glasgow

KEEP YOUR EYES on the stars, and your feet on the ground.—Theodore Roosevelt

Ideas

IF YOU WANT to get across an idea, wrap it up in a person.   —Ralph Bunche

NEVER, NEVER REST contented with any circle of ideas, but always be certain that a wider one is still possible.   —Richard Jefferies

YOU MUST FIND the ideas that have some promise in them . . . it is not enough to just have ideas, they must be finally ideas worth having and fruitful.
    —George E. Woodberry

LEARN TO LOVE ideas for themselves; and do not think, the instant a truth dawns on you, of devising a scheme for reforming the world.
    —John Lancaster Spalding

THE SECRET OF living is to find a pivot, the pivot of a concept on which you can make your stand.   —Luigi Pirandello

ABOVE ALL, DO not talk yourself out of good ideas by trying to expound them at haphazard gatherings.   —Jacques Barzun

A WRITER'S LIFE is his crucible. First you draw on your own experience. When you have drained your own experience or have stopped experiencing in quantity, you must draw on the experience of others through observation and research. Research is vital.   —Paddy Chayefsky

THE VITALITY OF thought is an adventure. *Ideas won't keep.* Something must be done about them. When the idea is new, its custodians have fervor, live for it, and if need be, die for it.   —Alfred North Whitehead

Illness

DESPISE NO NEW accident in your body, but ask opinion of it.—Francis Bacon

IN VISITING THE sick, do not presently play the physician if you be not knowing therein.

—George Washington

DO NOT SPEAK of thy bodily ailments to those who visit thee when thou art sick.

—Marcus Aurelius

DON'T LIVE IN a town where there are no doctors.

—Jewish proverb

> The surest road to health, say what they will,
> Is never to suppose we shall be ill.
> Most of those evils we poor mortals know
> From doctors and imagination flow.

—Charles Churchill

Imagination

THE FIRST OF our senses which we should take care never to let rust through disuse is that sixth sense, the imagination. . . . I mean the wide-open eye which leads us always to see truth more vividly, to apprehend more broadly, to concern ourselves more deeply, to be, all our life long, sensitive and awake to the powers and responsibilities given to us as human beings. —Christopher Fry

IMAGINATION IS THE ruler of our dreams—a circumstance that may account for the peculiar vividness of the impressions they produce. Let reason be the ruler of our waking thoughts.

—William Benton Clulow

LEARN TO FOSTER an ardent imagination; so shall you descry beauty which others passed unheeded.
—Norman Douglas

THE WORLD OF reality has its limits; the world of imagination is boundless. Not being able to enlarge the one, let us contract the other; for it is from their difference that all the evils arise which render us unhappy.
—Jean Jacques Rousseau

IMAGINE FOR YOURSELF a character, a model personality, whose example you determine to follow, in private as well as in public.
—Epictetus

ALWAYS BE ON guard against your imagination. How many lions it creates in our paths, and so easily! And we suffer so much if we do not turn a deaf ear to its tales and suggestions.
—George Porter

YOU CAN'T DEPEND on your judgment when your imagination is out of focus.
—Mark Twain

WORKS OF IMAGINATION should be written in very plain language; the more purely imaginative they are the more necessary it is to be plain.
—Samuel Taylor Coleridge

Immortality

WORK FOR IMMORTALITY if you will, than wait for it.
—Josiah G. Holland

LET US NOT be uneasy then about the different roads we may pursue, as believing them the shortest, to that our last abode, but following the guidance of a good conscience, let us be happy in the hope that by these different paths we shall all meet in the end.
—Thomas Jefferson

LET HIM WHO believes in immortality enjoy his happiness in silence, without giving himself airs about it. —Goethe

BE SURE THAT it is not you that is mortal, but only your body. For that man whom your outward form reveals is not yourself; the spirit is the true self, not that physical figure which can be pointed out by your finger. —Cicero

Impossibility

DO NOT THINK that what is hard for thee to master is impossible for man; but if a thing is possible and proper to man, deem it attainable by thee.

—Marcus Aurelius

BY ASKING FOR the impossible obtain the best possible. —Italian proverb

NEVER SAY NEVER, for if you live long enough, chances are you will not be able to abide by its restrictions. . . . In 1921 I told myself and millions of fans, that I would never marry again. I have had four husbands since then. . . . Never is a long, undependable time, and life is too full of rich possibilities to have restrictions placed upon it. —Gloria Swanson

HOPE NOT FOR impossibilities. —Thomas Fuller

DON'T BATHE IF there is no water. —Shan proverb

NOTHING IS IMPOSSIBLE; there are ways that lead to everything, and if we had sufficient will we should always have sufficient means. It is often merely for an excuse that we say things are impossible. —François de La Rochefoucauld

Individuality/Originality

INSIST ON YOURSELF; never imitate. Your own gift you can present every moment with the cumulative force of a whole life's cultivation; but of the adopted talent of another, you have only an extemporaneous half-expression. That which each can do best none but his Maker can teach him.

—Ralph Waldo Emerson

IF A MAN does not keep pace with his companions, perhaps it is because he hears a different drummer. Let him step to the music that he hears, however measured or far away.

—Henry David Thoreau

WHAT ANOTHER WOULD have done as well as you, do not do it. What another would have said as well as you, do not say it. What another would have written as well, do not write it. Be faithful to that which exists nowhere but in yourself—and thus make yourself indispensable. —André Gide

RESOLVE TO BE thyself; and know that he who finds himself loses his misery. —Matthew Arnold

FOLLOW YOUR OWN bent, no matter what people say. —Karl Marx

LET ALL YOUR views in life be directed to a solid, however moderate, independence; without it no man can be happy, nor even honest. —Junius

KNOW THEN THAT the world exists for you. . . . All that Adam had, all that Caesar could, you have and can do. Adam called his house heaven and earth; Caesar called his house Rome; you perhaps call yours a cobbler's trade, a hundred acres of ploughed land, or a scholar's garret. Yet line for line and point for point your dominion is as great as theirs, though without fine names. Build therefore your own world. —Ralph Waldo Emerson

Industry/Productivity

MY MESSAGE TO you is: Be courageous. I have seen many depressions in business. Always America has emerged from these stronger and more prosperous. Be brave as your fathers were before you. Have faith! Go forward! —Thomas Alva Edison

PRODUCE! PRODUCE! WERE it but the pitifullest infinitesimal fraction of a product, produce it in God's name! 'Tis the utmost thou has in thee: out with it, then. —Thomas Carlyle

. . . NEVER HARASS SOMEBODY . . . working at his capacity. A mediocre person I never harass. I believe most people don't know what they can do. Look, what's the difference between Vince Lombardi and a high school football coach? They both know the same plays. It's a question of getting a little more precision.

—Henry Kissinger

IF YOU WANT work well done, select a busy man—the other kind has no time.

—Elbert Hubbard

Influence

NO MAN SHOULD think himself a zero, and think he can do nothing about the state of the world.

—Bernard M. Baruch

EACH AND EVERY one of us has one obligation, during the bewildered days of our pilgrimage here: the saving of his own soul, and secondarily and incidentally thereby affecting for good such other souls as come under our influence.

—Kathleen Norris

YOU CAN EXERT no influence if you are not susceptible to influence.

—C. G. Jung

LET HIM THAT would move the world first move himself.

—Socrates

Initiative

Cast thy bread upon the waters:
For thou shalt find it after many days.

—Old Testament

IF THERE IS no wind, row.

—Latin proverb

IT IS THE greatest of all mistakes to do nothing because you can do only a little. Do what you can.

—Sydney Smith

HAVE YOU GOT a problem? Do what you can where you are with what you've got.

—Theodore Roosevelt

Insult

I'VE ALWAYS FOLLOWED my father's advice: He told me, first, to always keep my word and, second, to never insult anybody unintentionally. If I insult you, you can be goddamn sure I intend to. And, third, he told me not to go around looking for trouble.

—John Wayne

HE WHO PUTS up with insult invites injury.

—Jewish proverb

THE WAY TO procure insults is to submit to them: A man meets with no more respect than he exacts.

—William Hazlitt

IF A DONKEY bray at you, don't bray at him.

—George Herbert

Integrity

NEVER ESTEEM ANYTHING as of advantage to thee that shall make thee break thy word or lose thy self-respect.

—Marcus Aurelius

BE SO TRUE to thyself as thou be not false to others.

—Francis Bacon

This above all; to thine own self be true
And it must follow, as the night the day,
Thou canst not then be false to any man.

>—Polonius, in Shakespeare's
>*Hamlet Prince of Denmark*

To be persuasive, we must be believable.
To be believable, we must be credible.
To be credible, we must be truthful.

>—Edward R. Murrow

BE HONEST WITH yourself until the end of your life. Then listen to the slow movement of the Schubert Quintet and kick the bucket.—Nathan Milstein, at age 77

Intellect

SEEK YE FIRST the good things of the mind, and the rest will either be supplied or its loss will not be felt.   —Francis Bacon

WE SHOULD TAKE care not to make the intellect our god; it has, of course, powerful muscles, but no personality.   —Albert Einstein

MEASURE YOUR MIND'S height by the shade it casts.   —Robert Browning

IF YOU WOULD stand well with a great mind, leave him with a favorable impression of yourself; if with a little mind, leave him with a favorable impression of himself.   —Samuel Taylor Coleridge

PREPARE YOURSELF FOR the great world, as the athletes used to do for their exercises; oil your mind and your manners, to give them the necessary suppleness and flexibility; strength alone will not do, as young people are too apt to think.

—Lord Chesterfield

IF YOUR HEAD is wax, don't walk in the sun.

—Benjamin Franklin

A MAN SHOULD keep his little brain attic stocked with all the furniture that he is likely to use, and the rest he can put away in the lumber-room of his library, where he can get it if he wants it.

—Sir Arthur Conan Doyle

RULE YOUR MIND or it will rule you.

—Horace

Interests

YOU MUST LEARN day by day, year by year, to broaden your horizon. The more things you love, the more you are interested in, the more you enjoy, the more you are indignant about—the more you have left when anything happens.

—Ethel Barrymore

ONE THING LIFE taught me: if you are interested, you never have to look for new interests. They come to you. When you are genuinely interested in one thing, it will always lead to something else.

—Eleanor Roosevelt

THERE IS SO little time for the discovery of all that we want to know about the things that really interest us. We cannot afford to waste it on the things that are only of casual concern for us, or in which we are interested only because other people have told us that we ought to be.

—Alec Waugh

A GREAT PRESERVATIVE against angry and mutinous thoughts, and all impatience and quarreling, is to have some great business and interest in your mind, which, like a sponge shall suck up your attention and keep you from brooding over what displeases you.

—Joseph Rickaby

Introspection

By all means use sometimes to be alone.
Salute thy self: see what thy soul doth wear.
Dare to look in thy chest, for 'tis thine own:
And tumble up and down what thou find'st there.
    Who cannot rest till he good-fellows finde,
    He breaks up house, turns out of doores his minde.

—George Herbert

WE SHOULD EVERY night call ourselves to an account: What infirmity have I mastered today? what passions opposed? what temptation resisted? what virtue acquired? Our vices will abate of themselves if they are brought every day to the shrift.

—Seneca

LOOK WELL INTO thyself; there is a source of strength which will always spring up if thou wilt always look there.

—Marcus Aurelius

TURNING ATTENTION TO oneself in the earnest endeavor to improve one-self may only increase obsession with oneself, which is the root of the mischief. . . . To be whole persons we must get ourselves off our hands.

—Harry Emerson Fosdick

Intuition/Instinct

WHEN MAKING A decision of minor importance I have always found it advantageous to consider all the pros and cons. In vital matters, however, such as the choice of a mate or a profession, the decisions should come from the unconscious, from somewhere within ourselves. In the important decisions of our personal lives we should be governed by the deep inner needs of our nature.

—Sigmund Freud

THE UNCONSCIOUS PART of your brain never stops working. So when you're faced with a perplexing job, work on it as hard as you can. Then, if you can't lick it, try sleeping on it or taking a walk or relaxing with friends. If you have primed yourself with all available facts, the answer is likely to "dawn" on you while your mind is seemingly at rest. . . . How can you develop your intuitive powers? Like any other form of thinking, intuition requires an alertness, sensitivity and discipline of mind which have to be cultivated. . . . Intuition isn't the enemy, but the ally, of reason.

—John Kord Lagemann

NEVER USE INTUITION.

—General Omar N. Bradley

ALL OUR PROGRESS is an unfolding like the vegetable bud. You have first an instinct, then an opinion, then a knowledge, as the plant has root, bud and fruit. Trust the instinct to the end, though you can render no reason.

—Ralph Waldo Emerson

LET HIM MAKE use of instinct who cannot make use of reason.

—From *Ray's English Proverbs*

Involvement

Trust no future, howe'er pleasant;
Let the dead past bury its dead;
Act—act in the living present,
Heart within, and God o'erhead.

—Henry Wadsworth Longfellow

YOU CAN'T ACHIEVE anything without getting in someone's way. You can't be detached and effective.
—Abba Eban

DO NOT PUT your spoon into the pot which does not boil for you.
—Roumanian proverb

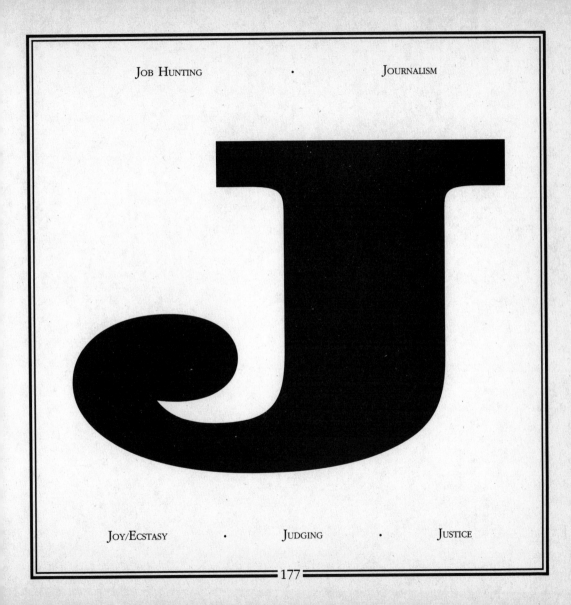

JOB HUNTING · JOURNALISM

JOY/ECSTASY · JUDGING · JUSTICE

Job Hunting

WRITING A RÉSUMÉ: Spend time on self-assessment first. Identify all the achievements of your past that illustrate skills. Describe them in active verbs and look for consistencies. That's the clue as to what you should emphasize. A résumé is scanned, not read. It's a sales tool that should give someone a sampling, not details in full.

—Jean Clarkson

YOU'RE NOT MAKING a social call when you apply for a job, so don't be cozy. Comments about the office furnishings or what the interviewer is wearing are inappropriate. In the same vein, don't be too confiding. The question, "Are you married?" requires only a yes or no, not a recital of your divorce action. Play it safe when you dress. Wear stockings; don't wear a pants suit; go easy on the makeup and perfume and hairdo. Be clean—if you can't decide whether or not a dress looks fresh enough to wear one more time, it doesn't.   —Barbara Walters

(1) REGARD JOB-HUNTING as a real job—and expect that it, like any other job, demands time, persistence and discipline. (2) Recognize that while you can get a good job through ads or employment agencies, competition for jobs that are advertised tends to be fierce. (3) Apply directly to an employer, even without any hint there's a job opening. Positions constantly become available and it's wise to be on a good list. (4) Try to get as many job interviews as you can and concentrate on smaller firms. (5) If you can see a layoff coming, start looking for a job while you are still working. (6) Expect to be discouraged. Guard against anger, apathy or feeling defeated.   —Sylvia Porter

Journalism

THERE IS NOT a crime, there is not a vice which does not live in secrecy. Get these things out in the open, describe them, attack them, ridicule them in the press and sooner or later public opinion will sweep them away.—Joseph Pulitzer

CAUTION TO A YOUNG REPORTER: Be wary. If your mother says she loves you, check on it.
—Ed Eulenberg

THE FUNCTION OF a good reporter is not to cover a story, but to uncover it. . . . Don't forget that the only two things people read in a story are the first and last sentences. Give them blood in the eye on the first one.—Herbert Bayard Swope

GET FIRST NAMES.
—I. A. Diamond

THE FIRST LAW of journalism, which is information gathering, should be: ask. Right? Not exactly. The First Law is listen. The Second Law is: ask. The Third Law is: pay attention to what you see, so you'll know what to ask. —Leonard Koppett

GUIDELINES FOR BEING a better reader, listener or viewer: Mix your mediums: Don't depend on a single source for your news. Compare the accounts. . . . Read, listen and view the news every day. . . . Read critically. . . . Seek out opposing views. (Broaden yourself by understanding the views of others). . . . Don't be headline happy. (There's a lot of news behind the headlines). . . . Read and listen intently. Watch for qualifying words and source limitations. Don't accept charge as conviction, rumor as fact or plan for accomplishment, reliable source as authority.
—Harland W. Warner

WHEN WE HEAR news we should always wait for the sacrament of confirmation.
—Voltaire

Joy/Ecstasy

All who joy would win
Must share it,
Happiness was born a twin.

—Lord Byron

WHEN YOU JUMP for joy beware that no one moves the ground from beneath your feet.
—Stanislaw Lec

SEIZE FROM EVERY moment its unique novelty and do not prepare your joys.
—André Gide

EAT WITH THE rich, but go to play with the poor, who are capable of joy.
—Logan Pearsall Smith

Judging

JUDGE NOT, THAT ye be not judged. For with what judgment ye judge, ye shall be judged: and with what measure ye mete, it shall be measured to you again. And why beholdest thou the mote that is in thy brother's eye, but considerest not the beam that is in thine own eye? Or how wilt thou say to thy brother, "Let me pull out the mote out of thine eye"; and, behold, a beam is in thine own eye? Thou hypocrite, first cast out the beam out of thine own eye, and then shalt thou see clearly to cast out the mote out of thy brother's eye.
—Jesus of Nazareth

JUDGE THYSELF WITH the judgment of sincerity, and thou will judge others with the judgment of charity. —John Mitchell Mason

DO NOT WAIT for the last judgment. It takes place every day. —Albert Camus

MAKE IT A PRACTICE to judge persons and things in the most favorable light at all times and under all circumstances. —Saint Vincent de Paul

DON'T MIND ANYTHING that anyone tells you about anyone else. Judge everyone and everything for yourself. —Henry James

LEAVE HER TO heaven.

—Ghost, in Shakespeare's
Hamlet Prince of Denmark

NEVER BE A judge between thy friends in any matter where both set their hearts upon the victory. If strangers or enemies be litigants, whatever side thou favorest, thou gettest a friend, but when friends are the parties thou losest one. —Jeremy Taylor

EVERY BIOGRAPHER SHOULD write on the first page of his manuscript: Thou shalt not judge. Moral judgment may be hinted at; but as soon as it is formulated, the reader is recalled to the sphere of ethics and the sphere of esthetics is lost to him. —André Maurois

Justice

IF THOU DESIRE rest unto thy soul, be just. . . . He that doth no injury, fears not to suffer injury; the unjust mind is always in labor; it either practices the evil it hath projected, or projects to avoid the evil it hath deserved.—Francis Quarles

BE JUST BEFORE you are generous. —Richard Brinsley Sheridan

THE POSSIBILITY THAT we may fail in the struggle ought not to deter us from the support of a cause we believe to be just. —Abraham Lincoln

IT IS ALWAYS wise, as it is also fair, to test a man by the standards of his own day, and not by those of another. —Odell Shepard

Knowledge

Kindness

GUARD WELL WITHIN yourself that treasure, kindness. Know how to give without hesitation, how to lose without regret, how to acquire without meanness. —George Sand

NO MAN IS so poor as to have nothing worth giving. . . . Give what you have. To someone it may be better than you dare to think.—Henry Wadsworth Longfellow

TO BE HAPPY you must forget yourself. Learn benevolence; it is the only cure of a morbid temper. —Edward George Bulwer-Lytton

DO NOT WAIT for extraordinary circumstances to do good; try to use ordinary situations. —Jean Paul Richter

FORGET INJURIES, NEVER forget kindnesses.   —Confucius

SHALL WE MAKE a new rule of life from tonight: always to try to be a little kinder than is necessary?
—James Matthew Barrie

START SOME KIND word on its travels. There is no telling where the good it may do will stop.
—Sir Wilfred Grenfell

HAVE YOU HAD a kindness shown? Pass it on.   —Henry Burton

BE KIND—REMEMBER every one you meet is fighting a battle—everybody's lonesome.
—Marion Parker

Knowledge

A little learning is a dangerous thing;
Drink deep, or taste not the Pierian spring;
There shallow draughts intoxicate the brain,
And drinking largely sobers us again.
—Alexander Pope

GRADUALNESS, GRADUALNESS AND gradualness. From the very beginning of your work, school yourself to severe gradualness in the accumulation of knowledge. . . . In gaining knowledge you must accustom yourself to the strictest sequence. You must be familiar with the very groundwork of science before you try to climb the heights. Never start on the "next" before you have mastered the "previous."
—Ivan Pavlov

IF YOU HAVE knowledge, let others light their candles at it.   —Margaret Fuller

IN A FREE world, if it is to remain free, we must maintain, with our lives if need be, but surely by our lives, the opportunity for a man to learn anything.

—J. Robert Oppenheimer

DO WHAT YOU know and perception is converted into character.

—Ralph Waldo Emerson

I HOPE THAT you have . . . gained an understanding of the limitations of knowledge. Knowledge, no matter how much it may transform the individual, is, in the end, not enough. . . . Science cannot now, and perhaps never will be able to, give us a complete account of our ultimate nature, or that of the physical environment in which we live.

—Harold J. Shapiro

Labor

THANK GOD EVERY morning when you get up that you have something to do that day which must be done, whether you like it or not. Being forced to work, and forced to do your best, will breed in you temperance and self-control, diligence and strength of will, cheerfulness and content, and a hundred virtues which the idle never know. —Charles Kingsley

NEVER STAND BEGGING for that which you have the power to earn.

—Miguel de Cervantes

WORK AND THOU canst not escape the reward; whether thy work be fine or coarse, planting corn or writing epics, so only it be honest work, done to thine own approbation, it shall earn a reward to the senses as well as to the thought. No matter how often defeated, you are born to victory. The reward of a thing well done is to have done it. —Ralph Waldo Emerson

REMEMBER, YOU HAVE to work. Whether you handle a pick or a pen, digging ditches or editing a paper, ringing an auction bell or writing funny things—you must work. If you look around, you will see the men who are the most able to live the rest of their days without work are the men who work the hardest. Don't be afraid of killing yourself with overwork. It is beyond your power to do that on the sunny side of thirty. So find out what you want to be, and do, and take off your coat, and make a dust in the world. —Charles Reade

IF YOU WISH to be at rest, labor. —Brother Giles of Assisi

DON'T BELIEVE THE world owes you a living; the world owes you nothing—it was here first.

—Robert Jones Burdette

(*See also* Advertising, Business, Management, and Work Psychology.)

Law

USE LAW AND physic only in cases of necessity; they that use them otherwise abuse themselves into weak bodies and light purses: they are good remedies, bad recreations but ruinous habits.

—Francis Quarles

DISCOURAGE LITIGATION. PERSUADE your neighbors to compromise whenever you can. . . . As a peace-maker the lawyer has a superior opportunity of being a good man. There will still be business enough.

—Abraham Lincoln

IF YOU HAVE a strong case in law, talk to the judge. If you have a strong case in fact, talk to the jury. But if you have no case in law or fact, talk to the wild elements and bellow like a bull.

—Judge Joe Baldwin

Do as adversaries do in law,
Strive mightily, but eat and drink as friends.

—Tranio, in Shakespeare's
The Taming of the Shrew

Leadership

IF YOU CRY "Forward!" you must without fail make plain in what direction to go. Don't you see that if, without doing so, you call out the word to both a monk and revolutionary, they will go in directions precisely opposite?—Anton Chekhov

I WOULD RATHER try to persuade a man to go along, because once I have persuaded him he will stick. If I scare him, he will stay just as long as he is scared, and then he is gone.   —Dwight D. Eisenhower

IN THIS WORLD no one rules by love; if you are but amiable, you are no hero; to be powerful, you must be strong, and to have dominion you must have a genius for organizing.   —John Henry Cardinal Newman

THE FIRST DUTY of a leader is to make himself be loved without courting love. To be loved without "playing up" to anyone—even to himself. —André Malraux

REMEMBER THAT IT is far better to follow well than to lead indifferently.
                                                                    —John G. Vance

LEARN TO OBEY before you command.   —Solon

                    What you cannot enforce,
                    Do not command.

                                                                  —Sophocles

AS SOON AS you are complicated, you are ineffectual.   —Maxim favored by
                                                              Konrad Adenauer

FIND OUT WHERE the people want to go, then hustle yourself around in front of them.
                                                              —James Kilpatrick

HE WHO RULES must humor fully as much as he commands.   —George Eliot

IF YOU WISH to know what a man is, place him in authority.—Yugoslav proverb

IT IS THE part of a good shepherd to shear his flock, not to skin it.
                                                                —Latin proverb

Learning

NEVER SEEM MORE learned than the people you are with. Wear your learning like a pocket watch and keep it hidden. Do not pull it out to count the hours, but give the time when you are asked. —Lord Chesterfield

STUDY, LEARN, BUT guard the original naivete. It has to be within you, as desire for drink is within the drunkard or love is within the lover.—Henri Matisse

HERE'S THE APPLE. My generation has already taken a bite out of it. But, like Adam, you have to make the best of an imperfect garden. What can you do? Two things: continue to learn and be sure to vote. First, learn. Inform yourselves. Read and think. Don't swallow what the newspapers print. Reflect continually about your government and who's running it, because they'll be doing it with your money. Second, vote. . . . How can you correct the follies of my generation unless you vote against them. . . . I would admonish you to stay keenly aware of hunger in this world and do what you can to overcome it. Behind great acts lie practical minds. —J. Peter Grace

IT IS NO profit to have learned well, if you neglect to do well.—Publilius Syrus

Letters

LET YOUR LETTER be written as accurately as you are able—I mean as to language, grammar, and stops; but as to the matter of it the less trouble you give yourself the better it will be. Letters should be easy and natural, and convey to the persons to whom we send just what we would say if we were with them. —Lord Chesterfield

IT'S BETTER TO send several short letters than one enormous thirty-page effort. . . . Don't wait for inspiration to come all at once. As events occur or when you read something stimulating, jot down a quick note about it and keep the notes and clippings with your writing paper. When you have a moment to write, you won't waste time trying to remember what you'd intended to say. Visualize the person you're writing to as if he or she were in the room with you. . . .

—Sheila Ostrander

WHEN A MAN sends you an impudent letter, sit right down and give it back to him with interest ten times compounded—and then throw both letters in the wastebasket.

—Elbert Hubbard

IF YOU ARE in doubt," says Talleyrand, "whether to write a letter or not—don't!" And the advice applies to many doubts in life besides that of letter-writing.

—Edward R. Bulwer-Lytton
(Pseudonym, Owen Meredith)

Life

Let us live then, and be glad,
While young life's before us;
After youthful pastime had,
After old age, hard and sad,
Earth will slumber o'er us.
(Gaudeamus igitur juvenes dum sumus
Post jucundam juventutem
Post molestam senectutem
Nos habebit humus.)

—Anonymous, *Gaudeamus Igitur*

REMEMBER THAT LIFE is neither pain nor pleasure; it is serious business, to be entered upon with courage and in a spirit of self-sacrifice. —Alexis de Tocqueville

NOR LOVE THY life, nor hate; but what thou livest, live well; how long or short permit to heaven. —John Milton

TRY AS MUCH as possible to be wholly alive, with all your might, and when you laugh, laugh like hell and when you get angry, get good and angry. Try to be alive. You will be dead soon enough. —William Saroyan

LET US NOT judge life by the number of breaths taken, but by the number of times the breath is held, or lost, either under a deep emotion, caused by love, or when we stand before an object of interest and beauty. —W. H. Davies

LIVE ALL YOU can; it's a mistake not to. It doesn't so much matter what you do in particular so long as you have your life. —Henry James

THE ART OF living is more like that of wrestling than of dancing; the main thing is to stand firm and be ready for an unforeseen attack. —Marcus Aurelius

LET US RUN with patience the race that is set before us. —New Testament

FEAR NOT THAT thy life shall come to an end, but rather fear that it shall never have a beginning. —John Henry Cardinal Newman

YOU CAN'T DO anything about the length of your life, but you can do something about its width and depth. —Evan Esar

LIFE IS SHORT; live it up. —Nikita S. Khrushchev

MAKE YOUR LIFE a mission—not an intermission. —Arnold Glasgow

We must live while live we can;
We should love while love we may.
—William Ernest Henley

SO LIVE THAT you wouldn't be ashamed to sell the family parrot to the town gossip. —Will Rogers

THE ART OF living lies not in eliminating but in growing with troubles.
—Bernard M. Baruch

Likeability

BE SINCERE. BE simple in words, manners and gestures. Amuse as well as instruct. If you can make a man laugh, you can make him think and make him like and believe you. —Alfred Emanuel Smith

DO YOU WANT to make friends? Be friendly. Forget yourself. . . . You can make more friends in two months by becoming interested in other people than you can in two years by trying to get other people interested in you.
—Dale Carnegie

BE REASONABLE: NO one can be perfect; he can only aim at being a likeable, reasonable being. —Lin Yutang

Limitations

IF THY STRENGTH will serve, go forward in the ranks; if not, stand still.

—Confucian proverb

CONSIDER WELL WHAT your strength is equal to, and what exceeds your ability.

—Horace

Run, if you like, but try to keep your breath;
Work like a man, but don't be worked to death.

—Oliver Wendell Holmes

DWELL NOT UPON thy weariness, thy strength shall be according to the measure of thy desire.

—Arab proverb

WRITERS! CHOOSE A subject equal to your abilities; think carefully what your shoulders may refuse and what they are capable of bearing.

—Horace

WHEN WE CANNOT get what we love, we must love what is within our reach.

—French proverb

Listening

THERE IS ONLY one rule for being a good talker—learn how to listen.

—Christopher Morley

WHEN PEOPLE TALK, listen completely. Most people never listen.

—Ernest Hemingway

EVERY MAN . . . SHOULD periodically be compelled to listen to opinions which are infuriating to him. To hear nothing but what is pleasing to one is to make a pillow of the mind. —St. John Ervine

LISTEN TO ALL, plucking a feather from every passing goose, but, follow no one absolutely. —Chinese proverb

KNOW HOW TO listen, and you will profit even from those who talk badly. —Plutarch

GROW ANTENNAE, NOT horns. —James B. Angell

Literary Composition

A GOOD RULE for writers; do not explain overmuch. —W. Somerset Maugham

THE IDEA IS to get the pencil moving quickly. . . . To write a scene, work up feeling: ride in on it. —Bernard Malamud

BE STILL WHEN you have nothing to say; when genuine passion moves you, say what you've got to say, and say it hot. —D. H. Lawrence

WHEN I AM working on a book or a story, I write every morning as soon after first light as possible. There is no one to disturb you and it is cool or cold and you come to your work and warm as you write. . . . When you stop you are as empty, and at the same time never empty but filling as when you have made love to someone you love. Nothing can hurt you, nothing can happen, nothing means anything until the next day when you do it again. It is the wait until the next day that is hard to get through. —Ernest Hemingway

READ, READ, READ. Read everything—trash, classics, good and bad, and see how they do it. Just like a carpenter who works as an apprentice and studies the mast. Read! You'll absorb it. Then write. If it is good, you'll find out. If it's not, throw it out the window.
—William Faulkner

ALL THIS ADVICE from senior writers to establish a discipline—always to get down a thousand words a day whatever one's mood—I find an absurdly puritanical and impractical approach. Write, if you must, because you feel like writing, never because you feel you *ought* to write.
—John Fowles

REVISE AND REVISE and revise—the best thought will come after the printer has snatched away the copy.
—Michael Monahan

I THINK IT'S a pretty good rule not to tell what a thing is about until it's finished. If you do you always seem to lose some of it. It never quite belongs to you so much again.
—F. Scott Fitzgerald

I SEE BUT one rule: to be clear. If I am not clear, all my world crumbles to nothing.
—Stendhal to Honoré de Balzac

''GET BLACK ON white'' used to be Maupassant's advice—that's what I always do. I don't give a hoot what the writing's like, I write any sort of rubbish which will cover the main outlines of the story, then I can begin to see it.
—Frank O'Connor

TO A BEGINNER, the advice I would give would be to think straight and write simply. To be clear is the first duty of a writer; to charm and to please are graces to be acquired later.
—Brander Matthews

JUST GET IT down on paper, and then we'll see what to do with it.
—Maxwell Perkin's advice to Marcia Davenport

ADVICE TO YOUNG writers who want to get ahead without any annoying delays: don't write about Man, write about a man. —E. B. White

THERE IS ONLY one way to defeat the enemy, and that is to write as well as one can. The best argument is an undeniably good book. —Saul Bellow

YOU HAVE TO assume that the act of writing is the most important of all. If you start worrying about people's feelings then you get nowhere at all.

—Norman Mailer

Learn the right
Of coining words in the quick mint of
joy.

—Leigh Hunt

GET AN AGENT. Make no excuses for the failure to do so. Get an agent. Otherwise you're a babe among wolves. —Brendan Francis

I HAD MARKED down in my notebook three characteristics a work of fiction must possess in order to be successful:

1. It must have a precise and suspenseful plot.
2. The author must feel a passionate urge to write it.
3. He must have the conviction, or at least the illusion, that he is the only one who can handle this particular theme. —Isaac Bashevis Singer

Interviewer: How many drafts of a story do you do?

THIRTY-SEVEN. I ONCE tried doing thirty-three, but something was lacking, a certain—how shall I say?—*je ne sais quoi*. On another occasion, I tried forty-two versions, but the final effect was too lapidary—you know what I mean, Jack? What the hell are you trying to extort—my trade secrets? —S. J. Perelman

WRITE WITHOUT PAY until somebody offers pay. If nobody offers pay within three years, the candidate may look upon this circumstance with the most implicit confidence as the sign that sawing wood is what he was intended for.

—Mark Twain

THE SECRET OF playwriting can be given in two maxims: stick to the point, and whenever you can, cut. —W. Somerset Maugham

(*See also* Writing.)

Little Things

DO NOT DELUDE yourself with the notion that you may be untrue and uncertain in trifles and in important things the contrary. Trifles make up existence, and give the measure by which to try us; and the fearful power of habit after a time, suffers not the best will to ripen into action. —Baron Karl Maria von Weber

DESPISE NOT SMALL things, either for evil or good, for a look may work thy ruin, or a word create thy wealth. A spark is a little thing, yet it may kindle the world. —Martin Farquhar Tupper

DO WELL THE little things now; so shall great things come to thee by and by asking to be done. —Persian proverb

NO MATTER HOW trifling the matter on hand, do it with a feeling that it demands the best that is in you, and when done look it over with a critical eye, not sparing a strict judgment of yourself. —Sir William Osler

DON'T BE AFRAID to give your best to what seemingly are small jobs. Every time you conquer one it makes you that much stronger. If you do the little jobs well, the big ones will tend to take care of themselves. —Dale Carnegie

Loneliness

THE BEST REMEDY for those who are afraid, lonely, or unhappy is to go outside, somewhere where they can be quite alone with the heavens, nature and God. Because only then does one feel that all is as it should be and that God wishes to see people happy amidst the simple beauty of nature. —Anne Frank

PRAY THAT YOUR loneliness may spur you into finding something to live for, great enough to die for. —Dag Hammarskjold

WE OUGHT NOT to isolate ourselves, for we cannot remain in a state of isolation. Social intercourse makes us the more able to bear with ourselves and with others. —Goethe

WHAT THEN IS the lonely person to do? . . . He must not be passive, waiting on the sidelines for someone to rescue him. Nor must he allow himself to be absorbed by the crowd. He should not count on being carried along in singles bars, group sex, political demonstrations or on following the current trends and opinions of others. . . . A lonely person cannot, then, wait for friends to assemble around and take care of him. Friendship, for each of us, begins with reaching out. . . . It always hurts to try to be a friend to man. It wears us down and wears us out, but it is still more rewarding and healthier to choose the active role rather than the passive one. . . . When a person asks that age-old question, "What can I do about my terrible loneliness?" The best answer is still, "Do something for somebody else." —Ann Landers, crediting Dr. Eugene Kennedy

Love (Romantic)

LET YOUR MISTRESS become accustomed to you and your curious ways, for the most potent thing in life is habit. Be with her on all occasions until you notice that she is used to you and needs your presence. —Ovid

ONE MUST LEARN to love, and go through a good deal of suffering to get to it, like any knight of the grail, and the journey is always towards the other soul, not away from it. . . . To love you have to learn to understand the other, more than she understands herself, and to submit to her understanding of you. It is damnably difficult and painful, but it is the only thing which endures.—D. H. Lawrence

THE WAY TO love anything is to realize that it might be lost. —G. K. Chesterton

> Love moderately; long love doth so;
> Too swift arrives as tardy as too slow.
>
> —Friar Laurence, in Shakespeare's
> *Romeo and Juliet*

> Let thy love be younger than thyself
> Or thy affection cannot hold the bent:
> For women are as roses; whose fair flower,
> Being once displayed, doth fall that very hour.
>
> —Orsino, the Duke, in Shakespeare's
> *Twelfth Night*

TAKE HOLD LIGHTLY; let go lightly. This is one of the great secrets of felicity in love. —Spanish proverb

NEVER PRETEND TO a love which you do not actually feel, for love is not ours to command. —Alan Watts

LET GRACE AND goodness be the principal loadstone of thy affections. For love which hath ends, will have an end; whereas that which is founded on true virtue, will always continue. —John Dryden

> Be good sweet maid,
> And let who will be naughty.
> If you grow better every day,
> How good you'll be at forty.
>
> —William Hazlitt

Love (Universal)

> Ah, love, let us be true
> To one another! for the world, which seems
> To lie before us like a land of dreams,
> So various, so beautiful, so new,
> Hath really neither joy, nor love, nor light,
> Nor certitude, nor peace, nor help for pain;
> And we are here as on a darkling plain
> Swept with confused alarms of struggle and flight,
> Where ignorant armies clash by night.
>
> —Matthew Arnold

THE BEST PRACTICAL advice I can give to the present generation is to practice the virtue which the Christians call love. —Bertrand Russell

He that shuts love out, in turn shall be
Shut out from love, and on her threshold lie
Howling in outer darkness.

—Alfred, Lord Tennyson

MAKE YOUR SERVICE of love a beautiful thing; want nothing else, fear nothing
else and let love be free to become what love truly is. —Hadewijch of Antwerp

Love (Unrequited)

TO FIND YOURSELF jilted is a blow to your pride. Do your best to forget it and
if you don't succeed, at least pretend to. —Molière

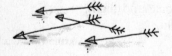

. . . if Harlequin steals your Columbine,
Laugh, Pagliaccio, and all will applaud you!

Change all your tears and anguish into clowning:
And into a grimace your sobbing and your pain . . .
Laugh, Pagliaccio, at your shattered love!
Laugh at the sorrow that has rent your heart!

—Canio, in Ruggiero Leoncavallo's
I Pagliacci

WHEN WE CAN'T have what we love we must love what we have.

—Roger de Bussy-Rabutin

Love (Wooing)

To get thine ends, lay bashfulness aside;
Who fears to ask, doth teach to be deny'd.

—Thomas Herrick

REMEMBER THE OLD saying: "Faint heart ne'er won fair lady."

—Miguel de Cervantes

If you want to win her hand
Let the maiden understand
That's she's not the only pebble on the beach.

—Harry Braisted

IF YOU WISH women to love you, be original. I know a man who used to wear fur hats summer and winter and women fell in love with him. —Anton Chekhov

SPEAK LOW IF you speak love.

—Don Pedro, in Shakespeare's
Much Ado About Nothing

Friendship is constant in all other things,
Save in the office and affairs of love:
Therefore, all hearts in love use their own tongues;
Let every eye negotiate for itself,
And trust no agent.

—Claudio, in Shakespeare's
Much Ado About Nothing

If thou must love me, let it be for naught
　　Except for love's sake only. Do not say,
　　'I love her for her smile—her look—her way
Of speaking gently—for a trick of thought
That falls in well with mine . . .'

But love me for love's sake, that evermore
　　Thou mayest love on, through love's eternity.

—Elizabeth Barrett Browning

Loyalty

UNLESS YOU CAN find some sort of loyalty, you cannot find unity and peace in your active living.
—Josiah Royce

REMEMBER THIS. IF you work for a man, in Heaven's name, work for him. If he pays you wages which supply you bread and butter, work for him; speak well of him; stand by him and stand by the institution he represents. If put to a pinch, an ounce of loyalty is worth a pound of cleverness. If you must vilify, condemn and eternally disparage—resign your position, and when you are on the outside, damn to your heart's content, but as long as you are part of the institution do not condemn it.
—Elbert Hubbard

THE SECRET OF a good life is to have the right loyalties and to hold them in the right scale of values.
—Norman Thomas

WHOEVER EATS MY bread sings my song.
—Harry Cohn

Luck

BE GRATEFUL FOR luck, but don't depend on it.
—William Feather

YOU KNOW WHAT luck is? Luck is believing you're lucky. Take at Salerno. I believed I was lucky. I figured that four out of five would not come through but I would . . . and I did. I put that down as a rule. To hold front position in this rat-race you've got to believe you are lucky.
—Stanley Kowalski, in Tennessee Williams's
A Streetcar Named Desire

WHENEVER YOU CAN, hang around the lucky.   —Jewish proverb

YOU CAN'T HOPE to be lucky. You have to prepare to be lucky.
                                                        —Timothy Dowd, N.Y.P.D.:
                                                           Deputy Inspector

GO AND WAKE up your luck.   —Persian proverb

MANAGEMENT · MANNERS · MARRIAGE · MATURITY · MEDICINE (HOME REMEDIES)

MELANCHOLY/THE BLUES · MEMORY · MERIT · METHOD · MIDDLE AGE

Management

NEVER TELL PEOPLE how to do things. Tell them *what* to do and they will surprise you with their ingenuity.
—George S. Patton

I CANNOT COMMEND to a business house any artificial plan for making men producers—any scheme for driving them into business-building. You must lead them through their self-interest. It is this alone that will keep them keyed up to the full capacity of their productiveness.
—Charles H. Steinway

DRIVE THY BUSINESS or it will drive thee.
—Benjamin Franklin

YOU'VE GOT TO do things differently when you get to a certain size or you're going to suffer.
—H. Brewster Atwater, Jr.

TRAIN UP A fig tree in the way it should go, and when you are old sit under the shade of it.
—Charles Dickens

RESPECT A MAN, he will do the more.
—James Howell

BEWARE OF THE man who won't be bothered with details.
—William Feather

NEVER WORK BEFORE breakfast; if you have to work before breakfast, get your breakfast first.
—Josh Billings

BREAK UP GOALS into small, manageable units. If entertaining is your problem, don't begin with a cocktail party. One person for lunch is just fine to start. If you can never take a vacation because no place seems perfect enough, go away for a weekend that is meant to be just that—a weekend, not the high point of your life.   —Suzanne McNear and David D. Burns, M.D.

IF IT WORKS, copy it.   —Tony Schwartz, describing a tenet
of successful prime-time programming

THE AIM OF the laborer should be, not to get his living, to get "a good job," but to perform well a certain work. Do not hire a man who does your work for money, but him who does it for love of it.   —Henry David Thoreau

(*See also* Advertising, Business, Labor, and Work Psychology.)

Manners

THERE ARE RULES of courteous behavior to be learned, fixed methods of procedure tested by long experience and handed down by tradition to make life more pleasant . . . Manners improve with practice . . . Don't be polite today, impatient and uncivil tomorrow; morose and sulky at home, affable at the office; obliging toward your friends and unfriendly toward strangers . . . Don't reserve your best behavior for special occasions. You can't have two sets of manners, two social codes—one for those you admire and want to impress, another for those whom you consider unimportant. You must be the same to all people.
—Lillian Eichler Watson

FOR MEN AND BOYS:

Do not—
    seat yourself while ladies are standing
    smoke without asking permission of a lady you are accompanying or sit so near (as in a train) that the smoke might annoy her

call any but your contemporaries, servants or children by their first names without their permission

keep your hat on while talking to a lady (unless asked to replace it) or fail to touch your hat or to lift it when necessary

nudge a woman or take her arm except to help her into and out of vehicles or across the street . . .

fail to pull out a lady's chair for her or fail to serve her or to see that she is served first

speak of repulsive matters at table.

—Amy Vanderbilt

ASSOCIATE WITH WELL-MANNERED persons and your manners will improve. Run around with decent folk and your own decent instincts will be strengthened. Keep the company of bums and you will become a bum. Hang around with rich people and you will end by picking up the check and dying broke.

—Stanley Walker

DON'T FLOP INTO the chair. *Insinuate* yourself. —Aunt in movie *Gigi*, 1958
Screenplay by Alan Jay Lerner

Marriage

IF YOU WOULD marry suitably, marry your equal.

—Ovid

Let there be spaces in your togetherness,
And let the winds of the heavens dance between you.
Love one another, but make not a bond of love:
Let it rather be a moving sea between the shores of your soul.
Fill each other's cup but drink not from one cup.
Give one another of your bread but eat not from the same loaf.
Sing and dance together and be joyous, but let each one of you be alone.
Even as the strings of a lute are alone though they quiver with the same music.

—Kahlil Gibran

NEVER MARRY BUT for love; but see that thou lovest what is lovely.

—William Penn

ONLY CHOOSE IN marriage a woman whom you would choose as a friend if she were a man.

—Joseph Joubert

LET HUSBAND AND wife infinitely avoid a curious distinction of mine and thine, for this hath caused all the laws, and all the suits, and all the wars in the world.
—Jeremy Taylor

NEVER GO TO bed mad. Stay up and fight.
—Phyllis Diller

ALL MARRIED COUPLES should learn the art of battle as they should learn the art of making love. Good battle is objective and honest—never vicious or cruel. Good battle is healthy and constructive, and brings to a marriage the principle of equal partnership.
—Ann Landers

ALWAYS REMEMBER, PEGGY, it's matrimonial suicide to be jealous when you have a really good reason.
—Clare Boothe Luce

YOU ARE LOOKING for a rich husband. At your age, I looked for hardship, danger, horror and death, that I might feel the life in me more intensely. I did not let the fear of death govern my life; and my reward was, I had my life. You are going to let the fear of poverty govern your life and your reward will be that you will eat, but you will not live.
—George Bernard Shaw

IF YOUR WIFE is small, stoop down and whisper in her ear.   —Jewish proverb

IF YOU MARRY, you will regret it. If you do not marry, you will also regret it.
—Soren Kierkegaard

WHENEVER YOU WANT to marry someone, go have lunch with his ex-wife.
—Shelley Winters

REMEMBER, THAT IF thou marry for beauty, thou bindest thyself all thy life for that which perchance will neither last nor please thee one year; and when thou hast it, it will be to thee of no price at all; for the desire dieth when it is attained, and the affection perisheth when it is satisfied. —Sir Walter Raleigh

DECEIVE NOT THYSELF by over-expecting happiness in the marriage state. . . . Marriage is not like the hill of Olympus, wholly clear, without clouds.

—Thomas Fuller

LOVE IS NOT enough. It must be the foundation, the cornerstone—but not the complete structure. It is much too pliable, too yielding. —Bette Davis

THERE IS NOTHING worse than solitude, growing old without a shoulder to lean on. Marry, marry—even if he's fat and boring! —Coco Chanel

Maturity

IN YOUR AMOURS you should prefer old Women to young ones . . . because they have more knowledge of the world and their Minds are better stored with Observations; their Conversation is more improving, and more lastingly agreeable. . . . Because when women cease to be handsome, they study to be good. To maintain their Influence over Man, they supply the Diminution of Beauty by an Augmentation of Utility. They learn to do a thousand Services, small and great, and are the most tender and useful of all Friends, when you are sick.

—Benjamin Franklin

''DON'T TRUST ANYONE over thirty!'' What ever happened to that asinine, divisive, and useless dictum so popular in the sixties? Answer: It has been unabashedly abandoned because its perpetrators are now themselves over thirty.

—Garson Kanin

TURN YOUR MIDLIFE crisis to your own advantage by making it a time for renewal of your body and mind, rather than stand by helplessly and watch them decline.
—Jane E. Brody

TO BE MATURE means to face, and not evade, every fresh crisis that comes.
—Fritz Kunkel

Medicine (Home Remedies)

STUDY SICKNESS WHEN you are well.
—Thomas Fuller

THE COMMON COLD: Rest in bed, hot drinks and aspirin. Nasal drops containing ephedrine can be used to relieve the running nose.
Prevention: At times when colds are prevalent, take plenty of citrus drinks.

Sore throat (mild form felt as an irritation or tickle): Hot lemon drinks, hot milk sweetened by honey, or gargling with salt.

Burns: Small burns should be covered with a cold, wet bandage. Do not open burn blisters. No oil and no ointment.
—Dr. Paul Kuhne, in the
Home Medical Encyclopedia

BETTER USE MEDICINES at the outset than at the last moment.—Publilius Syrus

Melancholy/The Blues

THE BEST CURE for worry, depression, melancholy, brooding, is to go deliberately forth and try to lift with one's sympathy the gloom of somebody else.
—Arnold Bennett

DRAG YOUR THOUGHTS away from your troubles—by the ears, by the heels, or any other way, so you manage it; it's the healthiest thing a body can do.

—Mark Twain

NEVER BEAR MORE than one trouble at a time. Some people bear three kinds—all they have had, all they have now, and all they expect to have.

—Edward Everett Hale

WORRIES GO DOWN better with soup than without.   —Jewish proverb

ALWAYS DIRECT YOUR thoughts to those truths that will give you confidence, hope, joy, love, thanksgiving, and turn away your mind from those that inspire you with fear, sadness, depression.   —Bertrand Wilberforce

When the melancholy fit shall fall . . .
Then glut thy sorrow on a morning rose.

—John Keats

WASTE NOT FRESH tears over old griefs.   —Euripides

LET TEARS FLOW of their own accord: their flowing is not inconsistent with inward peace and harmony.   —Seneca

GIVE NOT OVER thy soul to sorrow; and afflict not thyself in thy own counsel. Gladness of heart is the life of man and the joyfulness of man is length of days.

—Ecclesiasticus

Memory

WHEN YOU ARE being introduced to someone, pay close attention to the person's name. If you don't hear it clearly the first time, ask to have it repeated. Just the repeating of the name will make a lasting impression on your mind. You must hear it distinctly if you are going to remember it. Asking the spelling, such as: "Is it Hanson with an *e* or an *o?*" will also help lock it in your memory file. Try to picture the name just as you see the person's face. Test your memory after introduction. If you have met a number of people at a business or social gathering, try to identify each as you look around the room.

—Jean Laird, in
Executive Health Report

THE SECRET OF a good memory is attention, and attention to a subject depends upon our interest in it. We rarely forget that which has made a deep impression on our minds.
—Tryon Edwards

THE PALEST INK is better than the best memory.
—Chinese proverb

HE WHO IS not very strong in memory should not meddle with lying.
—Michel de Montaigne

PRAY FOR A short memory as to all unkindnesses.
—Charles E. Spurgeon

Merit

IF YOU WISH your merit to be known, acknowledge that of other people.

—Oriental proverb

DON'T LOOK FOR more honor than your learning merits. —Jewish proverb

> If you wish in this world to advance,
> Your merits you're bound to enhance;
> You must stir it and stump it,
> And blow your own trumpet,
> Or trust me, you haven't a chance.

—W. S. Gilbert

Method

BE METHODICAL IF you would succeed in business or in anything. . . . Whatever your calling, master all its bearings and details, its principles, instruments, and applications. Method is essential if you would get through your work easily and with economy of time. —William Matthews

IT IS NOT always by plugging away at a difficulty and sticking at it that one overcomes it; but, rather, often by working on the one next to it. Certain people and certain things require to be approached on an angle. —André Gide

A PLAUSIBLE TECHNIQUE of breaking up a batting slump: My guess is that a player is told what he is doing wrong or shown movies or videotapes of himself as he strikes out or grounds out easily. I suggest that, instead, he be shown a short film of himself hitting home runs. . . . Why do I think it will work? It could be imitation, but a more likely effect should be eliminating some of the aversive effects of the slump.   —B. F. Skinner

ATTEMPT EASY TASKS as if they were difficult, and difficult as if they were easy; in the one case that confidence may not fall asleep, in the other that it may not be dismayed.   —Baltasar Gracian

Middle Age

UNFOLD, LEAF BY LEAF.
Become more and more intimate with life.
Ask no cold question of any joyous thing.
Go to all living things gently, listening for the wonder of the breath and the
    heartbeat.
Ask all successful and happy creatures for a clue.   —Stuart P. Sherman

GROW UP AS soon as you can. It pays. The only time you really live fully is from thirty to sixty. . . . The young are slaves to dreams; the old servants of regrets. Only the middle-aged have all their five senses in keeping of their wits.
                                         —William Hervey Allen

I'M VERY PLEASED with each advancing year. It stems back to when I was forty. I was a bit upset about reaching that milestone, but an older friend consoled me. "Don't complain about growing old—many, many people do not have that privilege."
                                    —Chief Justice Earl Warren

Misfortune

WHENEVER EVIL BEFALLS us, we ought to ask ourselves, after the first suffering, how we can turn it into good. So shall we take occasion, from one bitter root, to raise perhaps many flowers.

—Leigh Hunt

> Once in Persia reigned a king
> Who upon his signet ring
> Graved a maxim true and wise,
>
> Solemn words, and these are they,
> "Even this shall pass away."

—Theodore Tilton

REFLECT ON YOUR present blessings, of which every man has many; not on your past misfortunes, of which all men have some.

—Charles Dickens

LEARN TO SEE in another's calamity the ills which you should avoid.

—Publilius Syrus

DO NOT PURSUE what is illusory—property and position: all that is gained at the expense of your nerves decade after decade and can be confiscated in one fell night. Live with a steady superiority over life—don't be afraid of misfortune, and do not yearn after happiness; it is, after all, all the same: the bitter doesn't last forever, and the sweet never fills the cup to overflowing.

—Alexander Solzhenitsyn

Mistake

ASSERT YOUR RIGHT to make a few mistakes. If people can't accept your imperfections, that's their fault. —David M. Burns, M.D.

BE NOT ASHAMED of mistakes and thus make them crimes.—Confucian proverb

I REMEMBER A very good bit of advice Fred used to give me right before we'd do a number: "Don't be nervous, but don't make any mistakes."
—Barrie Chase, talking about her dancing partner Fred Astaire

BETTER ASK TWICE than go wrong once. —German proverb

WHEN YOU MAKE a mistake, don't look back at it long. Take the reason of the thing into your mind, and then look forward. Mistakes are lessons of wisdom. The past cannot be changed. The future is yet in your power. —Hugh White

IF YOU HAVE made mistakes, even serious mistakes, there is always another chance for you. And supposing you have tried and failed again and again, you may have a fresh start any moment you choose, for this thing that we call "failure" is not the falling down, but the staying down. —Mary Pickford

LOOK UPON THE errors of others in sorrow, not in anger.
—Henry Wadsworth Longfellow

(*See also* Rightness.)

Moderation

NEVER GO TO excess, but let moderation be your guide. . . . Whatever you undertake, there are three rules to be observed. In the first place, it is necessary to subject appetite to reason, for that is the surest means of fulfilling your duty; again, you must estimate the importance of the object you wish to accomplish that the effort you bestow upon it may be neither greater nor less than the case demands. Finally, observe moderation in all that concerns the aspect and dignity of a gentleman; and moderation is best attained by observing . . . decorum . . . and never transgressing its limits. But the most important of these three rules is to subject appetite to reason.

—Cicero

Live so that you tempt not the sea relentless
Neither press too close on the shore forbidding . . .
Thus in stormy days be of heart courageous
And when waves are calm, and the danger over,
Wise man, trim your sails when a gale too prosp'rous
    Swells out the canvas.

—Horace

Let moderation on thy passions wait
Who loves too much, too much the lov'd will hate.

—Robert Herrick

Money

GET ALL YOU can, and what you can get hold; 'Tis the stone that will turn all your lead into gold. . . . Remember that money is of a prolific generating nature. Money can beget money, and its offspring can beget more. . . .

—Benjamin Franklin

NEVER SPEND YOUR money before you have it. —Thomas Jefferson

BE YOU IN what line of life you may, it will be amongst your misfortunes if you have not time properly to attend to . . . pecuniary matters. Want of attention to these matters has impeded the progress of science, and of genius itself. . . . To be poor and independent, is very nearly an impossibility. . . . This shame of being thought poor . . . leads to everlasting efforts to disguise one's poverty; the carriage, the servants, the wine (oh, that fatal wine!), the spirits, the decanters, the glasses, all the table apparatus, the dress, the horses, the dinners, the parties, all must be kept up; not so much because he or she who keeps or gives them derives any pleasure arising therefrom, as because not to keep and give them, would give rise to a suspicion of the want of means so to give and keep; and thus thousands upon thousands are yearly brought into a state of real poverty by their great anxiety not to be thought poor.
Mark it well; resolve to set this false shame at defiance, and when you have done

that, you have laid the first stone of the surest foundation of your future tranquility of mind.

—William Cobbett

PUT NOT YOUR trust in money, but put your money in trust.

—Oliver Wendell Holmes

IF EVER YOU have a lump of money large enough to be of any use, and can spare it, don't give it away: find some needed job that nobody is doing and get it done.

—George Bernard Shaw

MAKE ALL YOU can, save all you can, give all you can.

—John Wesley

LET ALL YOUR views in life be directed to a solid, however moderate, independence; without it no man can be happy, nor even honest.

—Junius

MY BOY . . . ALWAYS try to rub up against money, for if you rub up against money long enough, some of it may rub off on you.

—Damon Runyon

THE ART OF living easily as to money is to pitch your scale of living one degree below your means.

—Sir Henry Taylor

Have more than thou showest,
Speak less than thou knowest.

—Fool, in Shakespeare's
King Lear

UNDERSTAND YOURSELF, PROTECT yourself. And care enough to fight the hidden enemy of our system [economic ignorance] before it does indeed destroy us.

—Sylvia Porter

IF YOU WOULD have enemies, lend money to your friends.—Catalonian proverb

AMONGST ALL OTHER things of the world, take care of thy estate, which thou shalt ever preserve, if thou observe three things; first, that thou know what thou hast; what every thing is worth that thou hast; and to see that thou art not wasted by thy servants and officers.　　　　　—Sir Walter Raleigh, advice to his son, 1632

Morality

IN MORALS, ALWAYS do as others do; in art, never.　　　　　—Jules Renard

TO BE A saint is the exception; to be upright is the rule. Err, falter, sin, but be upright. To commit the least possible sin is the law for man. Sin is a gravitation.
　　　　　—The Bishop, in Victor Hugo's *Les Miserables*

BE NOT TOO hasty to trust or admire the teachers of morality; they discourse like angels, but they live like men.　　　　　—Samuel Johnson

DO NOT BE too moral. You may cheat yourself out of much life . . . Aim above morality. Be not simply good; be good for something.
　　　　　—Henry David Thoreau

IF YOUR MORALITY is joyless, try immorality, and have yourself some fun before they shove dirt in your face.　　　　　—Brendan Francis

IF YOUR MORALS make you dreary, depend on it, they are wrong.
　　　　　—Robert Louis Stevenson

Mortality

PERHAPS THE BEST cure for the fear of death is to reflect that life has a beginning as well as an end. There was a time when we were not; this gives us no concern—why then should it trouble us that a time will come when we shall cease to be?

—William Hazlitt

So live, that when thy summons comes to join
The innumerable caravan that moves
To the pale realms of shade, where each shall take
His chamber in the silent halls of death,
Thou go not, like the quarry-slave at night,
Scourged to his dungeon, but, sustained and soothed
By an unfaltering trust, approach thy grave
Like one who wraps the drapery of his couch
About him, and lies down to pleasant dreams.

—William Cullen Bryant

(*See also* Death.)

Motherhood

BEING A HOUSEWIFE and a mother is the biggest job in the world, but if it doesn't interest you, don't do it. . . . I would have made a terrible mother.

—Katharine Hepburn

A GIRL WHO wastes . . . her college years without acquiring serious interests and wastes her early job years marking time until she finds a man gambles with the possibilities for an identity of her own, as well as the possibilities for sexual fulfillment and wholly affirmed motherhood. The educators who encourage a woman to postpone larger interests until her children are grown make it virtually impossible for her ever to acquire them. It is not that easy for a woman who has defined herself wholly as wife and mother for ten or fifteen or twenty years to find new identity at thirty-five or forty or fifty. The ones who are able to do it are, quite frankly, the ones who made serious commitments to their earlier education, the ones who wanted and once worked at careers, the ones who bring to marriage and motherhood a sense of their own identity—not those who somehow hope to acquire it later on.   —Betty Friedan

THINK CAREFULLY ABOUT having that baby. Not to have it would be a great loss. To have it too late greatly increases the health hazards for you and the child. To have it without a commitment to it would be a great tragedy.

—Beverly Sills

Music

TAKE A MUSIC bath once or twice a week for a few seasons, and you will find that it is to the soul what the water bath is to the body. —Oliver Wendell Holmes

WHEN YOU WISH actively to increase your skill in listening and your understanding, however, devote some time, no matter how short, to *attentive* listening. . . . Listen repeatedly. Become familiar with the melodies, preferably to the point where you are able to sing them, but at least familiar enough for you to recognize them. Then watch for their growth and transformations. As you develop your skill in listening, let your ears wander; do not listen only to the "top." Listen to the bass part and to the parts in the middle. At concerts, watching the conductor as he "cues in" the instruments will often give you suggestions as to which instruments have the most important part. Do not expect to hear everything; more is offered than can possibly be grasped.   —David Randolph

IF WE WERE all determined to play the first violin we should never have a full ensemble. Therefore respect every musician in his proper place.

—Robert Schumann

WHETHER YOU LISTEN to Mozart or Duke Ellington, you can deepen your understanding of music only by being a more conscious and aware listener—not someone who is just listening, but someone who is listening for something.

—Aaron Copland

THE IMPORTANT THING is to feel your music, *really* feel it and *believe* it.

—Ray Charles

FIRST YOU HAVE to know *how* to do what you want to do with a particular song. Then there's the next step, which is turning the song into your own.

—Judy Collins

N

Nature

CLIMB THE MOUNTAINS and get their good tidings. Nature's peace will flow into you as sunshine flows into trees. The winds will blow their own freshness into you, and the storms their energy, while cares will drop away from you like the leaves of Autumn.

—John Muir

YOU MUST NOT know too much, or be too precise or scientific about birds and trees and flowers and watercraft; a certain free margin, and even vagueness—perhaps ignorance, credulity—helps your enjoyment of these things.

—Walt Whitman

TO ENJOY SCENERY you should ramble amidst it; let the feelings to which it gives rise mingle with other thoughts; look round upon it in intervals of reading;

and not go to it as one goes to see the lions fed at a fair. The beautiful is not to be stared at, but to be lived with. —Thomas Babington Macaulay

LIVE EACH SEASON as it passes; breathe the air, drink the drink, taste the fruit, and resign yourself to the influences of each. —Henry David Thoreau

TREAT SPRING JUST as you would a friend you have not learned to trust.

—Ed Howe

Negotiation

KEEP STRONG, IF possible. In any case, keep cool. Have unlimited patience. Never corner an opponent, and always assist him to save his face. Put yourself in his shoes—so as to see things through his eyes. Avoid self-righteousness like the devil—nothing is so self-blinding. —B. H. Liddell Hart

BE CAREFUL THAT victories do not carry the seeds of future defeats.

—Ralph W. Sockman

IF YOU WANT to persuade people, show the immediate relevance and value of what you're saying in terms of meeting their needs and desires. . . . Successful collaborative negotiation lies in finding out what the other side really wants and showing them a way to get it, while you get what you want. —Herb Cohen

JAW-JAW IS better than war-war. —Sir Winston Churchill

Nonconformity

BE COURTEOUS, BE obliging, but don't give yourself over to be melted down for the benefit of the tallow trade. —George Eliot

MANY THINGS THAT come into the world are not looked into. The individual says, "My crowd doesn't run that way." I say, don't run with crowds.

—Robert Henri

TAKE THE COURSE opposite to custom and you will do well.

—Jean Jacques Rousseau

WHOSO WOULD BE a man, must be a nonconformist. He who would gather immortal palms must not be hindered by the name of goodness, but must explore if it be goodness. Nothing is at last sacred but the integrity of your own mind. —Ralph Waldo Emerson

Nonviolence

WHOSOEVER SHALL SMITE thee on thy right cheek, turn to him the other also.

—New Testament

A STRONG MAN must be militant as well as moderate. He must be a realist as well as an idealist. If I am to merit the trust invested in me by some of my race, I must be both of these things. This is why nonviolence is a powerful as well as a *just* weapon. If you confront a man who has been cruelly misusing you, and say "Punish me, if you will; I do not deserve it, but I will accept it, so that the world will know I am right and you are wrong," then you wield a powerful and a just weapon. This man, your oppressor, is automatically morally defeated, and if he has any conscience, he is ashamed. Whenever this weapon is used in a manner that stirs a community's, or a nation's, anguished conscience, then the pressure of public opinion becomes an ally in your just cause.—Dr. Martin Luther King, Jr.

IT IS BETTER to be violent, if there is violence in our hearts, than to put on the cloak of nonviolence to cover impotence.　　　　　　　　—Mohandas K. Gandhi

Now

Look to this day!
For it is life, the very life of life.

For yesterday is but a dream
And tomorrow is only a vision
But today well lived makes every yesterday a dream of happiness
And tomorrow a vision of hope.
Look well, therefore, to this day!
Such is the salutation of the dawn.

　　　　　　　　　　　　　　　　　　　　　　—Kalidasa

SOME THERE ARE that torment themselves afresh with the memory of what is past; others, again, afflict themselves with the apprehension of evils to come; and very ridiculously both—for the one does not now concern us, and the other not yet. . . . One should count each day a separate life.　　—Seneca

LOOK NOT MOURNFULLY into the Past. It comes not back again. Wisely improve the Present. It is thine. Go forth to meet the shadowy Future, without fear, and with a manly heart.　　　　　　　　—Henry Wadsworth Longfellow

LET'S HAVE A merry journey, and shout about how light is good and dark is not. What we should do is not *future* ourselves so much. We should *now* ourselves more. "*Now* thyself" is more important than "*Know* thyself." Reason is what tells us to ignore the present and live in the future. So all we do is make plans. We think that somewhere there are going to be green pastures. It's crazy. Heaven is nothing but a grand, monumental instance of future. Listen, *now* is good. *Now* is wonderful.

—Mel Brooks

OPINION · OPPORTUNITY

ORATORY · ORDER

Opinion

YOU ARE YOUNG, my son, and, as the years go by, time will change and even reverse many of your present opinions. Refrain therefore awhile from setting yourself up as a judge of the highest matters. —Plato

STAY AT HOME in your mind. Don't recite other people's opinions.
—Ralph Waldo Emerson

DO NOT THINK of knocking out another person's brains because he differs in opinion from you. It would be as rational to knock yourself on the head because you differ from yourself ten years ago. —Horace Mann

ACCUSTOM YOURSELF TO not knowing what your opinions are till you have blurted them out, and thus find out what they are. —John Jay Chapman

JUDGE MEN NOT by their opinions, but by what their opinions have made of them. —Georg Christoph Lichtenberg

I THINK WE ought always to entertain our opinions with some measure of doubt. I shouldn't wish people dogmatically to believe any philosophy, not even mine. —Bertrand Russell

CONTINUE TO EXPRESS your dissent and your needs, but remember to remain civilized, for you will sorely miss civilization if it is sacrificed in the turbulence of change. —Will Durant

Opportunity

There is a tide in the affairs of men,
Which, taken at the flood, leads on to fortune;
Omitted, all the voyage of their life
Is bound in shallows and in miseries.
On such a full sea are we now afloat;
And we must take the current when it serves,
Or lose our ventures.

—Brutus, in Shakespeare's
Julius Caesar

SEIZE OPPORTUNITY BY the beard, for it is bald behind.   —Bulgarian proverb

THE LESSON WHICH life repeats and constantly enforces is "look under foot."
You are always nearer the divine and the true sources of your power than you
think. The lure of the distant and the difficult is deceptive. The great opportunity
is where you are. Do not despise your own place and hour. Every place is under
the stars, every place is the center of the world.   —John Burroughs

A WISE MAN will make more opportunities than he finds.   —Francis Bacon

THE CHINESE USE two brush strokes to write the word "crisis." One brush
stroke stands for danger; the other for opportunity. In a crisis, be aware of the
danger—but recognize the opportunity.   —Richard M. Nixon

Oratory

SPEAK PROPERLY, AND in as few words as you can, but always plainly; for the end of speech is not ostentation, but to be understood. —William Penn

BE A CRAFTSMAN in speech that thou mayest be strong, for the strength of one is the tongue, and speech is mightier than all fighting. —*Maxims of Ptahhotep,* 3400 B.C.

> Mend your speech a little,
> Lest it may mar your fortunes.
>
> —Lear, in Shakespeare's
> *King Lear*

SAY WHAT YOU have to say and the first time you come to a sentence with a grammatical ending—sit down. —Sir Winston Churchill

WHAT IS PRESENTED as right must shine like gold; what is presented as wrong must be black as pitch. If you begin to talk of your complicated motives, you will only create confusion. —Arthur Koestler

(*See also* Public Speaking and Speaking.)

Order

HAVE A TIME and place for everything, and do everything in its time and place, and you will not only accomplish more, but have far more leisure than those who are always hurrying, as if vainly attempting to overtake time that had been lost. —Tryon Edwards

SET ALL THINGS in their own peculiar place, and know that order is the greatest grace.
—John Dryden

IT IS BEST to do things systematically, since we are only human, and disorder is our worst enemy.
—Hesiod

WATCH OUT FOR the fellow who talks about putting things in order! Putting things in order always means getting other people under your control.
—Denis Diderot

Painting

I DO NOT presume to explain how to paint, but only how to get enjoyment. . . . Buy a paint box and have a try. If you need something to occupy your leisure, to divert your mind from the daily round, to illuminate your holidays, do not be too ready to believe that you cannot find what you want here. Even at the advanced age of forty! . . . Be persuaded that the first quality that is needed is Audacity. . . . Just to paint is great fun. . . . Every day you may make progress. Every step may be fruitful. Yet there will stretch out before you an ever-lengthening, ever-ascending, ever-improving path. You know you will never get to the end of the journey. But this, so far from discouraging, only adds to the joy and glory of the climb. —Sir Winston Churchill

PUT ONESELF IN touch with each artist . . . enter into his point of view . . . see as far as possible with his eyes, and to estimate his work not for what it does *not* contain, but for what it does. In this way only can our appreciation of painting become catholic and intelligent. Then, we are no longer content to say "I know what I like," but "I know why I like"; and our likings are multiplied. . . . Thus may we enter into the life of the artist and reinforce our own lives.
—Charles H. Caffin

I PAINT A window just as I look out of a window. If a window looks wrong in a picture open, I draw the curtain and shut it, just as I would in my own room. One must act in painting as in life, directly. —Pablo Picasso

YOU CANNOT REFUSE a new face. You must accept a face as a face. And so with an oil painting. You can now see that when it came first to Matisse and then to the cubism of Picasso nothing was a bother to me. Yes, of course, it was a bother to me, but not the bother of a refusal. —Gertrude Stein

SOME OF YOU are satisfied with the first shape, or at most by the second or third that appears. Not thus wrestle the victors, the unvanquished painters who never suffer themselves to be deluded by all those treacherous shadow shapes; they persevere till nature at the last stands bare to their gaze, and her very soul is revealed.

—Honoré de Balzac

(*See also* Art.)

Parenthood

DON'T BE AFRAID to be boss. Children are constantly testing, attempting to see how much they can get away with—how far you will let them go—and they secretly hope you will not let them go too far. Be aware of this testing mechanism the next time you are locked in bitter debate with your teen-ager. And don't bug out when the crunch comes. . . . Accept the fact that there will be moments when your children will hate you. This is normal and natural. But how a child handles hate may determine whether he will go to Harvard or San Quentin.

—Ann Landers

YOU HAVE THE right to make mistakes in bringing up your own children: Blunder bravely! Go ahead and make your mistakes, but believe more bravely that, on the whole, you are doing a good job of raising your children.

You have a right to pursue your own career and interests. If you don't meet your own needs, you are not going to meet your [children's].

You have the right to be yourself. Allow your child to be himself, and you will raise a happy and psychologically healthy individual. The same reasoning applies to you as a parent. So raise your child in your own unique way. Have the courage to be yourself—as a husband, or a wife and, above all, as a parent!

—Fitzhugh Dodson

IF YOU WANT to see what children can do, you must stop giving them things.

—Norman Douglas

ON CHILDREN IN SPORTS: Beware of your own expectations. Avoid putting so much pressure on a child that the only thing he or she can do is fail. . . . Never compare your child to a professional athlete. . . . Find out what kind of person is shaping your kids.

—John Dockery

Parting

NEVER PART WITHOUT loving words to think of during your absence. It may be that you will not meet again in life.

—Jean Paul Richter

And must we part?
Well—if we must, we must—and in that case
The less said the better.

—Richard Brinsley Sheridan

Say "au revoir" but not "good-bye,"
Though past is dead, Love cannot die.

—Harry Kennedy

Let's not unman each other—part at once;
All farewells should be sudden, when forever,
Else they make an eternity of moments,
And clog the last sad sands of life with tears.

—Lord Byron

Passion

One pulse of passion—youth's first fiery glow—
Is worth the hoarded proverbs of the sage:
Vex not thy soul with dead philosophy;
Have we not lips to kiss with, hearts to love, and eyes to see?

—Oscar Wilde

ALWAYS REFUSE THE advice that passion gives.   —English proverb

Take heed lest passion sway
Thy judgment to do aught,
      which else free will
Would not admit.

—John Milton

IT IS EASIER to exclude harmful passions than to rule them, and to deny them admittance than to control them after they have been admitted.   —Seneca

MORTAL LOVERS MUST not try to remain at the first step; for lasting passion is the dream of a harlot and from it we wake in despair.   —C. S. Lewis
The Pilgrim's Regress

The Past

FINISH EACH DAY and be done with it. You have done what you could. Some blunders and absurdities no doubt crept in; forget them as soon as you can. Tomorrow is a new day; begin it well and serenely and with too high a spirit to be cumbered with your old nonsense. —Ralph Waldo Emerson

MAKE IT A rule of life never to regret and never to look back. Regret is an appalling waste of energy; you can't build on it; it's only good for wallowing in. —Katherine Mansfield

SHUT OUT ALL of your past except that which will help you weather your tomorrows. —Sir William Osler

DO NOT BE afraid of the past. If people tell you that it is irrevocable, do not believe them. —Oscar Wilde

YOU CAN'T TURN back the clock. But you can wind it up again. —Bonnie Prudden

> Wouldst shape a noble life? Then cast
> No backward glances toward the past,
> And though somewhat be lost and gone,
> Yet do thou act as one new born;
> What each day needs, that shalt thou ask,
> Each day will set its proper task.
>
> —Goethe

WE OUGHT NOT to look back unless it is to derive useful lessons from past errors, and for the purpose of profiting by dear bought experience.

—George Washington

WE THINK IN generalities, but we live in detail. To make the past live, we must perceive it in detail in addition to thinking of it in generalities.

—Alfred North Whitehead

RESPECT THE PAST in the full measure of its deserts, but do not make the mistake of confusing it with the present nor seek in it the ideals of the future.

—José Ingenieros

LET SLEEPING DOGS LIE.

—English proverb

LET SLEEPING DOGMAS LIE.

—American "proverb"

Patience

HAVE PATIENCE WITH all things, but chiefly have patience with yourself. Do not lose courage in considering your own imperfections but instantly set about remedying them—every day begin the task anew. —Saint Francis de Sales

NEVER THINK THAT God's delays are God's denials. Hold on; hold fast; hold out. Patience is genius. —Comte de Buffon

PATIENCE SERVES AS a protection against wrongs as clothes do against cold. For if you put on more clothes as the cold increases, it will have no power to hurt you. So in like manner you must grow in patience when you meet with great wrongs, and they will then be powerless to vex your mind.

—Leonardo da Vinci

BEWARE THE FURY of a patient man. —John Dryden

WAIT FOR THE first class jewels, Gigi. Hold on to your ideals.

—Aunt in movie *Gigi*, 1958
Screenplay by Alan Jay Lerner

(*See also* Forbearance.)

Patriotism

LET ALL THE ends thou aimest at be thy country's, thy God's and truth's. Be noble and the nobleness that lies in other men—sleeping but not dead—will rise in majesty to meet thine own. —Words carved on Union Station, Washington, D.C.

OUR COUNTRY! IN her intercourse with foreign nations, may she always be in the right; but our country, right or wrong. —Stephen Decatur, Toast, 1816

''OUR COUNTRY RIGHT or wrong.'' When right to be kept right. When wrong to be put right. —Carl Schurz, Speech, 1873

YOU'RE NOT TO be so blind with patriotism that you can't face reality. Wrong is wrong, no matter who does it or says it. —Malcolm X

A MAN'S FEET should be planted in his country, but his eyes should survey the world. —George Santayana

LET US SHOW ourselves Americans by showing that we do not want to go off in separate camps or grounds by ourselves, but that we want to co-operate with all other classes and all other groups in a common enterprise which is to release the spirits of the world from bondage—that is the meaning of democracy.

—Woodrow Wilson

ASK NOT WHAT your country can do for you, ask what you can do for your country. —John F. Kennedy

Perception

THE FIRST REQUIREMENT for the growth of the individual is that the person remain in touch with his own perceptions. No matter how different one's experience is from that of others, he must trust in the validity of his own senses if he is to evolve as a unique human being. Only the person can fully know what he sees, what he hears, and what he feels to be fundamentally true.

—Clark Moustakas

WORDS ARE THE raw material of knowledge and in fact of life. . . . When [the educated person] finds a false one he will reject it as convincingly as one of my favorite heroines of modern literature. This favorite heroine of mine is a little girl in an old cartoon in *The New Yorker* magazine. She is being force-fed by her mother, but is obviously rejecting whatever it is that is being offered her. Finally, in desperation, her mother says to her: "But dear, it's broccoli." At this, the little three-year-old girl in her high chair looks at her mother and replies: "I say it's spinach and I say the hell with it!" As you go through life, may you gradually come to the knowledge of the difference between broccoli and spinach and may you acquire the courage to challenge those who confuse the two.

—Benjamin A. Rogge

TO SEE WHAT is right, and not to do it, is want of courage, or of principle.

—Confucius

Perseverance

DO NOT, FOR one repulse, forego the purpose that you resolved to effect.

—Antonio, in Shakespeare's
The Tempest

PRESS ON: NOTHING in the world can take the place of perseverance. Talent will not; nothing is more common than unsuccessful men with talent. Genius will not; unrewarded genius is almost a proverb. Education will not; the world is full of educated derelicts. Persistence and determination alone are omnipotent.

—Calvin Coolidge

KEEP ON GOING and the chances are you will stumble on something, perhaps when you are least expecting it. I have never heard of anyone stumbling on something sitting down.

—Charles F. Kettering

YOU MUST KEEP sending work out; you must never let a manuscript do nothing but eat its head off in a drawer. You send that work out again and again, while you're working on another one. If you have talent, you will receive some measure of success—but only if you persist.

—Isaac Asimov

Perseverance/Tenacity

WHEN YOU ARE in any contest you should work as if there were—to the very last minute—a chance to lose it. This is battle, this is politics, this is anything.

—Dwight D. Eisenhower

'Tis a lesson you should heed,
Try, try again;

If at first you don't succeed,
Try, try again;
Then your courage should appear,
For, if you will persevere,
You will conquer, never fear;
Try, try again.

—W. E. Hickson

BEAR IN MIND, if you are going to amount to anything, that your success does not depend upon the brilliancy and the impetuosity with which you take hold, but upon the everlasting and sanctified bull-doggedness with which you hang on after you have taken hold. —Dr. A. B. Meldrum

LET ME TELL you the secret that has led me to my goal. My strength lies solely in my tenacity. —Louis Pasteur

Perspective

THE BEST AND safest thing is to keep a balance in your life, acknowledge the great powers around us and in us. If you can do that, and live that way, you are really a wise man. —Euripides

DO NOT MEASURE your loss by itself; if you do, it will seem intolerable; but if you will take all human affairs into account you will find that some comfort is to be derived from them. —Saint Basil

IF YOU LOOK at life one way, there is always cause for alarm.—Elizabeth Bowen

THE IMPORTANT THING
is to pull yourself up by your own hair

to turn yourself inside out
and see the whole world with fresh eyes. —Peter Weiss, *Marat Sade*

THOU CANST BEGIN a new life! See but things afresh as thou used to see them;
for in this consists the new life. —Marcus Aurelius

Persuasion

IF YOU WOULD persuade, you must appeal to interest rather than intellect.
—Benjamin Franklin

WHEN THE CONDUCT of men is designed to be influenced, persuasion, kind,
unassuming persuasion, should ever be adopted. It is an old and true maxim
that "a drop of honey catches more flies than a gallon of gall." So with men. If
you would win a man to your cause, first convince him that you are his sincere
friend. Therein is a drop of honey that catches his heart, which, say what he will,
is the great highroad to his reason, and which, once gained, you will find but
little trouble in convincing him of the justice of your cause, if indeed that cause
is really a good one. —Abraham Lincoln

Yet hold it more humane, more heav'nly, first,
By winning words to conquer willing hearts,
And make persuasion do the work of fear.

—John Milton

IF YOU HAVE an important point to make, don't try to be subtle or clever. Use a
pile driver. Hit the point once. Then come back and hit it again. Then hit it a
third time—a tremendous whack.
—Sir Winston Churchill, to the young Prince of Wales, on speech-making

Pets

CATS: THE MOST important thing for any cat owner to realize is the deep need that cats have for human friendship and communication. When they are deprived of these things, they withdraw, deeply hurt, and are accused of coldness and ingratitude. In legend and in fact, cats have proved to be every bit as loyal to their human friends as dogs have; and what is more, they talk to us. The tone of your voice, a surprising number of actual words, your gestures and caresses will soon put you in direct communication with your cat. . . . I suggest you start talking to your cat, or better still, to your kitten just as soon as you can. You can't begin too young. . . . The Siamese is the easiest cat to talk to. In my experience, the males, in particular, are garrulous to the extreme.　　—Patricia Moyes

DOGS: TO SUCCESSFULLY train a dog, the owner must maintain the cool objectivity of a "pro." This means not allowing frustrations to interfere with relating to the dog. . . . The dog must not be yelled at or punished in any way. If the owner has had a trying day he must either postpone the lesson or stay alert not to abuse the dog because he didn't get that promotion, or his wife dented a fender. . . . Forget the word *punishment*. Replace it with *correction*. . . . No training session should last longer than fifteen minutes. . . . Try to be extra patient and understanding during the first few sessions. He is going to be denied every impulse that is natural for him. It will be a whole new world of discipline and obedience. —Mordecai Siegal and Matthew Margolis

HORSES: WHEN APPROACHING a horse, whether from his front or his rear, always speak quietly to him to call his attention to you and your actions. Horses often doze with their eyes half open and may be thrown into a panic if they are unexpectedly touched. A quiet voice will give the horse enough warning to prepare him for your approach. —Sue Henderson Coen

Physicians

GO NOT FOR every grief to the physician, nor for every quarrel to the lawyer, nor for every thirst to the pot.

DECEIVE NOT THY physician, confessor or lawyer. —George Herbert

Use three physicians
Still: first, Dr. Quiet;
Next, Dr. Merryman,
And Dr. Dyet.
—*Regimen Sanitatis Salernitanum*, 1607 edition

PHYSICIAN, HEAL THYSELF. —New Testament, Luke IV

CARE MORE FOR the individual patient than for the special features of the disease. —Sir William Osler

YOU CAN ONLY cure retail but you can prevent wholesale. —Brock Chisholm

KEEP A WATCH also on the faults of the patients, which often make them lie about the taking of things prescribed. —Hippocrates

BEWARE OF THE young doctor and the old barber. —Benjamin Franklin

THE ETHICS OF LIFE-AND-DEATH DECISIONS: Pecca fortier. . . . Sin bravely. . . . We will never have all the facts to make a perfect judgment, but with the aid of basic experience we must leap bravely into the future.
—Russell R. McIntyre, bioethicist

STRIVE TO PRESERVE your health; and in this you will the better succeed in proportion as you keep clear of the physicians, for their drugs are a kind of alchemy concerning which there are no fewer books than there are medicines.
—Leonardo da Vinci

HONOR A PHYSICIAN with the honor due unto him. —Ecclesiasticus

Planning

HE WHO EVERY morning plans the transaction of the day and follows out that plan, carries a thread that will guide him through the maze of the most busy life. But where no plan is laid, where the disposal of time is surrendered merely to the chance of incidence, chaos will soon reign. —Victor Hugo

IN ACTION, BE primitive; in foresight, a strategist.
—René Char

EVERY TIME YOU have a task before you, examine it carefully, take exact measure of what is expected of you. Then make your plan and, in order to execute it properly, create for yourself a method, never improvise.
—Marshal Ferdinand Foch

LET OUR ADVANCE worrying become advance thinking and planning.
—Sir Winston Churchill

WHEN WE ARE planning for posterity, we ought to remember that virtue is not hereditary.
—Thomas Paine

NEVER TAKE ANYTHING for granted.
—Benjamin Disraeli

Pleasure

GET PLEASURE OUT of life . . . as much as you can. Nobody ever died from pleasure.
—Sol Hurok

Ever let the Fancy roam,
Pleasure never is at home.
—John Keats

WE MAY LAY in a stock of pleasures, as we would lay in a stock of wine; but if we defer tasting them too long, we shall find that both are soured by age.
—Charles Caleb Colton

I AM ADVISING you as a friend, as a man of the world, as one who would not have you old while you are young, but would have you take all the pleasures that reason points out, and that decency warrants. . . . Choose your pleasures for yourself, and do not let them be imposed upon you.   —Lord Chesterfield

TO MAKE PLEASURES pleasant, shorten them.   —Charles Buxton

Poetry

EVERY ENGLISH POET should master the rules of grammar before he attempts to bend or break them.   —Robert Graves

IN A POEM the words should be as pleasing to the ear as the meaning is to the mind.   —Marianne Moore

I WISH OUR clever young poets would remember my homely definitions of prose and poetry; that is, prose—words in their best order; poetry—the best words in their best order.   —Samuel Taylor Coleridge

POETRY SHOULD PLEASE by a fine excess and not by singularity. It should strike the reader as a wording of his own highest thoughts, and appear almost as a remembrance.   —John Keats

A POET SHOULD be treated with leniency and, even when damned, should be damned with respect.   —Edgar Allan Poe

Politics

BEFORE YOU CAN begin to think about politics at all, you have to abandon the notion that here is a war between good men and bad men. —Walter Lippmann

POLITICS IS LIKE football. If you see daylight, go through the hole.
—John F. Kennedy
(*See* "Sport," Vince Lombardi)

CARRY THE BATTLE to them. Don't let them bring it to you. Put them on the defensive. And don't ever apologize for anything.
—Harry S. Truman to Hubert H. Humphrey during the 1964 campaign

YOU CANNOT IN this game of politics fight your own party. It just doesn't work.
—Barry M. Goldwater

DON'T SACRIFICE YOUR political convictions for the convenience of the hour.
—Edward M. Kennedy

IT IS NOT the man who sits by his fireside reading his evening paper, and saying how bad are politics and politicians, who will ever do anything to save us; it is the man who goes out into the rough hurly-burly of the caucus, the primary, and the political meeting, and there faces his fellows on equal terms.
—Theodore Roosevelt

WHEN THE WATER reaches the upper level, follow the rats. —Claude Swanson

FORGIVE BUT NEVER forget.
—Attributed to John F. Kennedy
by Ted Sorensen

NEVER FORGET, RARELY forgive.
—Edward I. Koch

IF YOU WANT to get along, go along.
—Sam Rayburn

DON'T WORRY ABOUT polls—but if you do, don't admit it.
—Rosalynn Carter

NEVER MURDER A man who is committing suicide.
—Woodrow Wilson

NEVER HOLD DISCUSSIONS with the monkey when the organ grinder is in the room.
—Sir Winston Churchill

DON'T ROLL UP your pants legs before you get to the stream.—Emanuel Celler

WATCH WHAT WE do, not what we say.
—John Mitchell

IF IT AIN'T broke, don't fix it.
—Bert Lance

IF YOU CAN'T stand the heat, get out of the kitchen.
—Harry S Truman

IF YOU HAVE a weak candidate and a weak platform, wrap yourself up in the American flag and talk about the Constitution.
—Matt Quay

VOTE FOR THE man who promises least; he'll be the least disappointing.
—Bernard M. Baruch

OPEN EACH SESSION with a prayer and close it with a probe.—Clarence Brown

THERE IS ONE rule for politicians all over the world: Don't say in Power what you say in Opposition; if you do, you only have to carry out what the other fellows have found impossible.
—John Galsworthy

IF YOU CAN'T lick 'em—join 'em.   —Political proverb

YOU DON'T HAVE to destroy the city before you can build a new Jerusalem.
                                                                    —Lane Kirkland

LOOK OVER YOUR shoulder now and then to be sure someone's following you.
                                                                    —Henry Gilmer

NEVER TELL THEM what you wouldn't do.   —Adam Clayton Powell

WHEN SOMEONE WITH a rural accent says, "I don't know anything about politics," zip up your pockets.   —Donald Rumsfeld

DIRKSEN'S THREE LAWS OF POLITICS. (1) Get elected. (2) Get reelected. (3) Don't get mad, get even.   —Senator Everett Dirksen

Positive Thinking

BELIEVE IN YOURSELF! Have faith in your abilities! Without a humble but reasonable confidence in your own powers you cannot be successful or happy. . . . Formulate and stamp indelibly on your mind a mental picture of yourself as succeeding. Hold this picture tenaciously. Never permit it to fade. Your mind will seek to develop the picture. . . . Do not build up obstacles in your imagination. . . . Do not be awestruck by other people and try to copy them. Nobody can be you as efficiently as YOU can. Remind yourself that God is with you and nothing can defeat him.   —Norman Vincent Peale

IF YOU THINK you can win, you can win. Faith is necessary to victory.
                                                                    —William Hazlitt

DON'T BE DISCOURAGED by a failure. It can be a positive experience. Failure is, in a sense, the highway to success, inasmuch as every discovery of what is false leads us to seek earnestly after what is true, and every fresh experience points out some form of error which we shall afterwards carefully avoid.

—John Keats

BE LIKE THE bird, who halting in his flight on limb too slight, yet sings— knowing he has wings.

—Victor Hugo

THE WAY YOU overcome shyness is to become so wrapped up in something that you forget to be afraid.

—Lady Bird Johnson

THEY CAN DO all because they think they can.

—Virgil

THE MOST IMPORTANT thing in life is to see to it that you are never beaten.

—André Malraux

Power

"GIVE ME A standing place," said Archimedes, "and I will move the world."— Goethe has changed the postulate into the precept: "Make good thy standing place, and move the world."

—Samuel Smiles

DO NOT TALK to me of Archimedes' lever. He was an absent-minded person with a mathematical imagination. Mathematics command my respect, but I have no use for engines. Give me the right word and the right accent and I will move the world.

—Joseph Conrad

THE SECRET OF all power is—save your force. If you want high pressure you must choke off waste.

—Joseph Farrell

THE GREAT SECRET of power is never to will to do more than you can accomplish.
—Henrik Ibsen

THERE IS A homely adage which runs: "Speak softly and carry a big stick; you will go far."
—Theodore Roosevelt

LET NOT THY will roar, when thy power can but whisper.
—Thomas Fuller

EXERCISE YOURSELF IN what lies in your power.
—Epictetus

I BELIEVE IN the hold-your-nose theory of coalition building. Even if you can't stand to be in the same room with certain people, join together with them to gain more power and influence.
—Carol Bellamy

WE SHOULD TRY to bring to any power what we have as women. We will destroy it all if we try to imitate that absolutely unfeeling, driving ambition that we have seen coming at us from across the desk.
—Colleen Dewhurst

USE POWER TO curb power.
—Chinese proverb

FAR BETTER TO think historically, to remember the lessons of the past. Thus, far better to conceive of power as consisting in part of the knowledge of when not to use all the power you have. Far better to be one who knows that if you reserve the power not to use all your power, you will lead others far more successfully and well.
—A. Bartlett Giamatti
President, Yale University

Praise

WHENEVER YOU COMMEND, add your reasons for doing so; it is this which distinguishes the approbation of a man of sense from the flattery of sycophants and admiration of fools.
—Sir Richard Steele

DON'T BE CHARY of appreciation. Hearts are unconsciously hungry for it.
—Phillips Brooks

> Do what thy manhood bids thee do,
>   from none but self expect applause;
> He noblest lives and noblest dies who
>   makes and keeps his self-made laws.
> —Sir Richard Francis Burton

YOU DO ILL if you praise, but worse if you censure, what you do not understand.
—Leonardo da Vinci

NEVER MIND WHOM you praise, but be very careful whom you blame.
—Edmund Gosse

> Be thou the first true merit to befriend,
> His praise is lost who stays till all commend.
> —Alexander Pope

BE NOT EXTRAVAGANTLY high in expression of thy commendations of men thou likest, it may make the hearer's stomach rise.
—Thomas Fuller

NEVER PRAISE A sister to a sister, in the hope of your compliments reaching the proper ears.　　　　　　　　　　　　　　　—Rudyard Kipling

WHEN SOMEONE DOES something good, applaud! You will make two people happy.　　　　　　　　　　　　　　　—Samuel Goldwyn

(*See* also Criticism.)

Prayer

DO NOT PRAY for easy lives. Pray to be stronger men. Do not pray for tasks equal to your powers. Pray for powers equal to your tasks. Then the doing of your work shall be no miracle, but you shall be the miracle.　　—Phillips Brooks

PRAY AS IF everything depended upon God and work as if everything depended upon man.　　　　　　　　　　—Francis Cardinal Spellman

CALL ON GOD, but row away from the rocks.　　　　　　—Indian proverb

PRAY, PRAY VERY much; but beware of telling God what you want.
　　　　　　　　　　　　　　　—French proverb

THE TIME TO pray is not when we are in a tight spot but just as soon as we get out of it.　　　　　　　　　　　　　　—Josh Billings

> Pray for my soul. More things are wrought by prayer
> Than this world dreams of.
>
> 　　　　　　　　　　　—Alfred, Lord Tennyson

Prejudice

NEVER TRY TO reason the prejudice out of a man. It was not reasoned into him, and cannot be reasoned out.

—Sydney Smith

NEVER SUFFER THE prejudice of the eye to determine the heart.

—Johann Georg von Zimmermann

SHAKE OFF ALL the fears of servile prejudices, under which weak minds are servilely crouched. Fix reason firmly in her seat, and call on her tribunal for every fact, every opinion. Question with boldness even the existence of a God; because, if there be one, he must more approve of the homage of reason than that of blindfolded fear.

—Thomas Jefferson

Preparedness

THE SUPERIOR MAN, when resting in safety, does not forget that danger may come. When in a state of security he does not forget the possibility of ruin. When all is orderly, he does not forget that disorder may come. Thus his person is not endangered, and his States and all their clans are preserved.   —Confucius

For all your days prepare,
  And meet them all alike:
When you are the anvil, bear—
    When you are the hammer, strike.

—Edwin Markham

BE PREPARED.

—Boy Scout motto

TAKE TIME TO prepare. Ten years' preparation for preliminaries to architectural practice is little enough for any architect who would rise "above the belt" in true architectural appreciation or practice. Then go as far away as possible from home to build your first buildings. The physician can bury his mistakes, but the architect can only advise his client to plant vines. —Frank Lloyd Wright

TRAIN IN TIME of peace to maintain direction at night with the aid of a luminous dial compass. Train in difficult, trackless, wooded terrain. War makes extremely heavy demands on the soldier's strength and nerves. For this reason make heavy demands on your men in peacetime exercises.

—Field Marshal Erwin Rommel

Pride

MY PRIDE KEEPS me going. That's why I work so hard. . . . I was taught to play hard, though maybe I wasn't taught. I just watched my dad. I'm nothing more than my dad in the next generation. . . . He always took time when I needed it for constructive criticism. He didn't holler at me like some fathers. He just tried to explain the right ways. —Pete Rose

REMEMBER THE SPANISH knight of legend who was starving, yet each evening walked in the square showily picking his teeth as if after a copious repast.

—George Kent

FLOWERS NEVER EMIT so sweet and strong a fragrance as before a storm. When a storm approaches thee, be as fragrant as a sweet-smelling flower.

—Jean Paul Richter

NEVER THINK YOU know all. Though others may flatter you, retain the courage to say, "I am ignorant." Never be proud. And lastly, science must be your passion. —Ivan Pavlov

Procrastination

KNOW THE TRUE value of time; snatch, seize, and enjoy every moment of it. No idleness; no laziness; no procrastination; never put off till to-morrow what you can do to-day.
— Lord Chesterfield

NEVER DO TODAY what you can put off till tomorrow. Delay may give clearer light as to what is best to be done.
—Aaron Burr

Delay not till to-morrow to be wise;
To-morrow's sun to thee may never rise.

—William Congreve

"NEVER PUT OFF until tomorrow what you can do today." Under the influence of this pestilent morality, I am forever letting tomorrow's work slop backwards into today's, and doing painfully and nervously today what I could do quickly and easily tomorrow.
—J. A. Spender

Proficiency

IN ORDER TO have any success in life, or any worthy success, you must resolve to carry into your work a fullness of knowledge—not merely a sufficiency, but more than a sufficiency. Be fit for more than the thing you are now doing. Let every one know that you have a reserve in yourself; that you have more power than you are now using. If you are not too large for the place you occupy, you are too small for it.
—James A. Garfield

TRY TO PUT into practice what you already know; and in so doing, you will, in good time, discover the hidden things which you now inquire about. Practice what you know, and it will help to make clear what now you do not know.

—Rembrandt van Rijn

TO SEE SO far as one may, and to feel the great forces that are behind every detail—for that makes all the difference between philosophy and gossip—to hammer out as compact and solid a piece of work as one can, to try to make it first rate, and to leave it unadvertised.   —Oliver Wendell Holmes, Jr.

WHEN YOU ARE not practicing, remember, someone somewhere is practicing, and when you meet him he will win.   —Ed Macauley

Progress

REMEMBER! THINGS IN life will not always run smoothly. Sometimes we will be rising toward the heights—then all will seem to reverse itself and start downward. The great fact to remember is that the trend of civilization itself is forever upward, that a line drawn through the middle of the peaks and the valleys of the centuries always has an upward trend.   —Endicott Peabody

BEHOLD THE TURTLE. He makes progress only when he sticks his neck out.

—James Bryant Conant

THERE IS NO law of progress. Our future is in our own hands, to make or to mar. It will be an uphill fight to the end, and would we have it otherwise? Let no one suppose that evolution will ever exempt us from struggles. "You forget," said the Devil, with a chuckle, "that I have been evolving too."

—William Ralph Inge

Promises

NEVER PROMISE MORE than you can perform.　　　　　　—Publilius Syrus

A PROMISE MUST never be broken.　　　　　　—Alexander Hamilton

BETTER BREAK YOUR word than do worse in keeping it.　　—Thomas Fuller

MAGNIFICENT PROMISES ARE always to be suspected.　　—Theodore Parker

THE BEST WAY to keep one's word is not to give it.　　—Napoleon Bonaparte

Prosperity/Adversity

REMEMBER THAT THERE is nothing stable in human affairs; therefore avoid undue elation in prosperity, or undue depression in adversity.　　—Socrates

A FULL CUP must be carried steadily.　　　　　　—English proverb

WATCH LEST PROSPERITY destroy generosity.　　—Henry Ward Beecher

TAKE CARE TO be an economist in prosperity; there is no fear of your being one in adversity.　　　　　　—Johann Georg von Zimmermann

WHO FEELS NO ills, should, therefore, fear them; and when fortune smiles, be doubly cautious, lest destruction come remorseless upon him, and he fall unpitied.　　　　　　—Sophocles

THE TRICK IS to make sure you don't die waiting for prosperity to come.

—Lee Iacocca

Prudence

DRINK NOTHING WITHOUT seeing it; sign nothing without reading it.

—Spanish proverb

WHEN YOU GO to buy, use your eyes, not your ears. —Czech proverb

Be sure yourself and your own reach to know,
How far your genius, taste, and learning go;
Launch not beyond your depth, but be discreet,
And mark that point where sense and dullness meet.

—Alexander Pope

DO NOT TRUST all men, but trust men of worth; the former course is silly, the latter a mark of prudence. —Democritus

DO NOT TAKE things by the point. —W. Rance

LEAVE WELL—EVEN "pretty well"—alone: that is what I learn as I get old.

—Edward Fitzgerald

DON'T RUN TOO far; you will have to return the same distance.—Old Testament

REVEAL NOT EVERY secret you have to a friend, for how can you tell but that friend may hereafter become an enemy. And bring not all the mischief you are able to upon an enemy, for he may one day become your friend. —Saadi

NO CALL ALLIGATOR long mouth till you pass him. —Jamaican proverb

DO NOT EMPLOY handsome servants.

—Chinese proverb

DON'T STAY LONG when the husband is not at home.

—Japanese proverb

Public Service

HAVE I DONE anything for society? I have then done more for myself. Let that question and truth be always present to thy mind, and work without cessation.

—William G. Simms

YOU HAVE GOT to have the same interest in public affairs as in private affairs, or you cannot keep this country what this country should be.—Theodore Roosevelt

YOU WILL FIND that the mere resolve not to be useless, and the honest desire to help other people, will, in the quickest and delicatest ways, improve yourself.

—John Ruskin

FINISH WHAT YOU begin. Public confidence in government isn't guaranteed; it has to be earned. I know of no other way to earn the trust and cooperation of the public than first, to say what you intend to do, and the second, to do it.

—Neil Goldschmidt

Public Speaking

TO SWAY AN audience, you must watch them as you speak.   —C. Kent Wright

ALWAYS BE SHORTER than anyone dared to hope.   —Lord Reading

BE SINCERE; BE brief; be seated.   —Franklin D. Roosevelt

LET THY SPEECH be short,
Comprehending much in a few words. —Apocrypha

BE BRIEF, FOR no discourse can please when too long. —Miguel de Cervantes

BEGIN AT THE beginning and go on till you come to the end; then stop.
—The King, in Lewis Carroll's
Alice in Wonderland

CULTIVATE EASE AND naturalness. Have all your powers under command.
Take possession of yourself, as in this way only can you take possession of your
audience. If you are ill at ease, your listeners will be also. Always speak as
though there were only one person in the hall whom you had to convince. Plead
with him, argue with him, arouse him, touch him, but feel that your audience is
one being whose confidence and affection you want to win. —Charles Reade

EXAMINE WHAT IS said, not him who speaks. —Arabian proverb

IF YOU ARE speaking, forget everything but the subject. Never mind what
others are thinking of you or your delivery. Just forget yourself and go ahead.
—Dale Carnegie

IF YOU HAVEN'T struck oil in the first three minutes—stop boring!
—George Jessel

LET IT NEVER be said of you, "I thought he would never finish." Follow the
advice I was given when singing in supper clubs: "Get off while you're ahead;
always leave them wanting more." Make sure you have finished speaking before
your audience has finished listening. A talk, as Mrs. Hubert Humphrey reminded
her husband, need not be eternal to be immortal. —Dorothy Sarnoff

(*See also* Oratory and Speaking.)

Purpose

YOU ARE NOT here merely to make a living. You are here in order to enable the world to live more amply, with greater vision, with a finer spirit of hope and achievement. You are here to enrich the world, and you impoverish yourself if you forget the errand.
—Woodrow Wilson

HAVE A PURPOSE in life, and having it throw into your work such strength of mind and muscle as God has given you.
—Thomas Carlyle

THIS IS OUR purpose: to make as meaningful as possible this life that has been bestowed upon us; to live in such a way that we may be proud of ourselves; to act in such a way that some part of us lives on.
—Oswald Spengler

Q

QUESTIONABLE ADVICE

Quality/Value

NEVER BUY WHAT you do not want, because it is cheap; it will be dear to you.

—Thomas Jefferson

HOW TO IMPROVE goods and services? Learn to complain, politely and firmly, when you receive what you believe to be inferior goods or services. Don't register your complaint with the salesperson or the waiter, but with the boss or the owner. He'll listen.

YOU SHOULD BUY the best you can afford, not the poorest of what you can't. From the best quality you will get the most satisfaction, the longest wear and the enjoyment of knowing it is the best without having to apologize for it.

—Stanley Marcus

SURELY THERE COMES a time when counting the cost and paying the price aren't things to think about any more. All that matters is value—the ultimate value of what one does.

—James Hilton

Quarreling

NEVER FALL OUT with your bread and butter.

—English proverb

MAKE SURE TO be in with your equals if you're going to fall out with your superiors.

—Jewish proverb

Beware
Of entrance to a quarrel, but, being in,
Bear it that the opposed may beware of thee. . . .

—Polonius, in Shakespeare's
Hamlet Prince of Denmark

THE ADVICE OF a father to his son: "Beware of entrance to a quarrel, but, being in, bear it that the opposed may beware of thee," is good, and yet not the best. Quarrel not at all. No man resolved to make the most of himself can spare time for personal contention. Still less can he afford to take all the consequences, including the vitiating of his temper and loss of self control. Yield larger things to which you can show no more than equal right; and yield lesser ones, though clearly your own. Better give your path to a dog than be bitten by him in contesting for the right. Even killing the dog would not cure the bite.

—Abraham Lincoln, in a letter to J. M. Cutts, October 26, 1863

Questionable Advice

THE ONLY WAY to get rid of a temptation is to yield to it. Resist it, and your soul grows sick with longing for the things it has forbidden to itself.   —Oscar Wilde

IF THE PATH be beautiful, let us not ask where it leads.   —Anatole France

> Don't steal; thou'lt never thus compete
> Successfully in business. Cheat.
>
>   —Ambrose Bierce

EATING WHILE SEATED makes one large of size; eating while standing makes one strong.   —Hindu proverb

USE YOUR HEALTH, even to the point of wearing it out. That is what it is for. Spend all you have before you die; and do not outlive yourself.

—George Bernard Shaw

THE MAN WHO makes an appearance in the business world, the man who creates personal interest, is the man who gets ahead. Be liked and you will never want.   —Willy Loman, in Arthur Miller's *Death of a Salesman*

IF YOU WOULD have the good will of all men, take heed that, when anything is asked of you, you don't refuse it pointblank, but answer in generalities.

—Francesco Guicciardini

IF A NEIGHBOR chokes, put a glass of water within reach . . . and do not watch.   —Debrett's *Etiquette and Modern Manners*

DO NOT LEARN more than you absolutely need to get through life.—Karl Kraus

UNJUST LAWS EXIST; shall we be content to obey them, or shall we endeavor to amend them, and obey them until we have succeeded, or shall we transgress them at once? . . . If the injustice is part of the necessary friction of the machine of government, let it go, let it go; perchance it will wear smooth . . . but if it is of such a nature that it requires you to be the agent of injustice to another, then, I say, break the law. Let your life be a counter-friction to stop the machine. What I have to do is to see, at any rate, that I do not lend myself to the wrong which I condemn.

—Henry David Thoreau

LET THINGS WORK themselves out. . . . The order of nature is proud and it is pitiless. Our fears, our despairs disgust it, and only keep it from coming to our aid, instead of inviting it. It owes its source to illness as well as to health. Bribes for the one and against the other, it will not take. That is confusion. Follow the order of nature, for God's sake! Follow it! It will lead who follows; and those who will not, it will drag along anyway, and their tempers and their medicines with them. Get a purge for your brain. It will do better for you than for your stomach.

—Michel de Montaigne

> Let's live with that small pittance we have;
> Who covets more is evermore a slave.
>
> —Thomas Herrick

DO NOT TROUBLE yourself much to get new things, whether clothes or friends. Turn the old; return to them. Things do not change; we change.

—Henry David Thoreau

WHEN YOU'VE GOT it—flaunt it.

—George Lois

IMMENSE POWER IS acquired by assuring yourself in your secret reveries that you were born to control affairs.

—Andrew Carnegie

Q

WELCOME EVERYTHING THAT comes to you, but do not long for anything else.
> —André Gide

DAMN PRINCIPLE! STICK to your party.
> —Benjamin Disraeli

DRINK! FOR YOU know not whence you came, nor why:
Drink! For you know not why you go, nor where.
> —Omar Khayyam

IF YOU STRIKE a child, take care that you strike it in anger, even at the risk of maiming it for life. A blow in cold blood neither can nor should be forgiven.
> —George Bernard Shaw

TO WRITE A good love letter, you ought to begin without knowing what you mean to say, and to finish without knowing what you have written.
> —Jean Jacques Rousseau

GET WHAT YOU can and keep what you have; that's the way to get rich.
> —Scottish proverb

FOUR FIFTHS OF all our troubles in this life would disappear, if we would only sit down and keep still. . . .

In the discharge of the duties of the office, there is one rule of action more important than all others. It consists in never doing anything that someone else can do for you.
> —Calvin Coolidge

CHOOSE NONE FOR thy servant who have served thy betters. —George Herbert

WHAT YOU CAN'T have, abuse.
> —Italian proverb

(*See also* Bad Advice, Counsel, Facetious Advice, and Fatherly Advice.)

Reading

READ NOT TO contradict and confute; nor to believe and take for granted; nor to find talk and discourse; but to weigh and consider. Some books are to be tasted, others to be swallowed, and some few to be chewed and digested: that is, some books are to be read only in parts, others to be read, but not curiously, and some few to be read wholly, and with diligence and attention. . . . Reading makes a full man, conference a ready man, and writing an exact man.

—Francis Bacon

RESOLVE TO EDGE in a little reading every day, if it is but a single sentence. If you gain fifteen minutes a day, it will make itself felt at the end of the year.

—Horace Mann

LET NOT THE authority of the writer offend thee whether he be of great or small learning; but let the love of pure truth draw thee to read.—Thomas à Kempis

FORCE YOURSELF TO reflect on what you read, paragraph by paragraph.

—Samuel Taylor Coleridge

BE SURE THAT you go to the author to get at *his* meaning, not to find yours.

—John Ruskin

READING, AFTER A certain age, diverts the mind too much from its creative pursuits. Any man who reads too much and uses his own brain too little falls into lazy habits of thinking.

—Albert Einstein

IF I AM at all partial, it is to the man who reads rapidly. One of the silliest couplets ever composed is to be found in "The Art of Reading," by one William Walker, a seventeenth-century hollow-head who wrote:

Learn to read slow; all other graces
Will follow in their proper places.

This is unmitigated balderdash and if taken seriously can easily result in the wasting of ten or fifteen per cent of the few waking hours God has put at our disposal.
—Clifton Fadiman

LET US READ with method, and propose to ourselves an end to which our studies may point. The use of reading is to aid us in thinking. —Edward Gibbon

WE MUST FORM our minds by reading deep rather than wide.
—Marcus Fabius Quintilianus

Reality

SET UP AS an ideal the facing of reality as honestly and as cheerfully as possible.
—Dr. Karl Menninger

THE REAL WORLD is not easy to live in. It is rough; it is slippery. Without the most clear-eyed adjustments we fall and get crushed. A man must stay sober: not always, but most of the time.
—Clarence Day

A TOUGH LESSON in life that one has to learn is that not everybody wishes you well.
—Dan Rather

I HOPE THAT young dramatists will realize that reality is not bounded by the bedsheets, that people have brains as well as genitals, that life is often more important than lust, and that gentleness and wisdom are not luxuries but necessities.
—Lord (Ted) Willis

Reason

NEVER REASON FROM what you do not know. If you do, you will soon believe what is utterly against reason. —Andrew M. Ramsay

IT IS USELESS to attempt to reason a man out of a thing he was never reasoned into. —Jonathan Swift

NEVER GET ANGRY. Never make a threat. Reason with people.
—Don Corleone, in Mario Puzo's
The Godfather

Recreation

IT IS THE part of a wise man to feed himself with moderate pleasant food and drink and to take pleasure with perfumes, with the beauty of growing plants, dress, music, sports, and theaters. —Benedict Spinoza

CHOOSE SUCH PLEASURES as recreate and cost little. —Thomas Fuller

WHEN YOU PLAY, play hard; when you work, don't play at all.
—Theodore Roosevelt

BELIEVE ME, MY young friend, there is *nothing*—absolutely nothing—half so much worth doing as simply messing about in boats. —Kenneth Grahame

(*See also* Pleasure and Rest/Relaxation.)

Regretting

"HENRY," I SAID, "we've done it." I said: "Remember Lot's wife. Never look back." I don't know whether Henry [Kissinger] had read the Old Testament or not, but I had, and he got the point. Henry and I often had a little joke between us after that. Whenever he would come in and say, "Well, I'm not sure we should have done this, or that, or the other thing," I would say, "Henry, remember Lot's wife." And that would end the conversation.   —Richard M. Nixon

YOU CANNOT GO around and keep score. If you keep score on the good things and the bad things, you'll find out that you're a very miserable person. God gave man the ability to forget, which is one of the greatest attributes you have. Because if you remember everything that's happened to you, you generally remember that which is the most unfortunate.   —Hubert H. Humphrey

MAKE THE MOST of your regrets. . . . To regret deeply is to live afresh.
                    —Henry David Thoreau

Relationships (Man/Woman)

A MAN IS talking to you, nothing very personal. Look into his eyes as though tomorrow's daily double winners were there. Never let your eyes leave his. . . . This look has been referred to rather disdainfully as "hanging on his every word." It was good in your grandmother's day and it's still a powerhouse! (Is there any comparison between this and gazing all around the room to see if anybody good just came in?)   —Helen Gurley Brown

ACCORDING AS THE man is, so must you humour him.   —Terence

WHEN A WOMAN is talking to you, listen to what she says with her eyes.

—Victor Hugo

THE MODERN RULE is that every woman should be her own chaperon.

—Amy Vanderbilt

AFTER THE RELATIONSHIP HAS ENDED: Feel what you are feeling. Mourn. Take time to think about yourself. Denying what you feel doesn't work. Figure out what you have learned by being in this relationship. Only then will you be free to move on.
—Dr. Elaine Hatfield

TO THOSE SUFFERING FROM A BROKEN RELATIONSHIP: Give yourself something you always wanted, not what you need. Indulge yourself in some way—it helps to restore your self-esteem.
—Dr. Lee Salk

AFTER AN UNHAPPY MARRIAGE OR RELATIONSHIP: Before you get involved, sexually and emotionally, be sure you know whom you're getting involved with. If a man says: "I like you, but I don't want to get involved," believe him. Don't think you can change him, or you will certainly get burned.

FOR THOSE WHO WANT A RELATIONSHIP TO CONTINUE: Communicate. Negotiate. Compromise. You must be able and willing to change. You must be able to consider another person's needs. You must talk with each other, not just guess what your partner is thinking. What else are words for? —Dr. Hanna Kapit

Relatives

IN-LAW SITUATIONS: The two most difficult situations to meet happily and successfully are those between the husband and his father-in-law and between the wife and her mother-in-law. The other relationships are easy and there is little reason for failure. In any case, the very first rule that every father-in-law—and especially every mother-in-law—must learn is DON'T INTERFERE. Never mind what small blunders your daughter or daughter-in-law or your son or son-in-law may make; remember that it is their right to live and do and think as they please. If you are asked what you think, answer truthfully, of course, but don't pour good advice upon them.

—Elizabeth L. Post

BEWARE OF A man's shadow [his relations] and a bee's sting.—Burmese proverb

NEVER RELY ON the glory of the morning nor the smiles of your mother-in-law.

—Japanese proverb

Go to friends for advice;
To women for pity;
To strangers for charity;
To relatives for nothing.

—Spanish proverb

Religion

IF YOU CAN'T have faith in what is held up to you for faith, you must find things to believe in yourself, for a life without faith in something is too narrow a space to live.

—George E. Woodberry

THERE ARE TWO techniques that every man and woman needs to live life. One is the technique of volition, of trying hard, putting your back into it and doing your best. That's *output*. . . . The other is the philosophy of intake, of spiritual hospitality, of the receptivity of the soul to the oversoul, of the open door that lets the highest in. That's *intake*. One is like the branches of a tree, spreading out. The other is like roots, digging in. Multitudes of people in our modern world are using only the first technique. They are trying hard, and then some-day, inevitably, like everybody else, they run into an experience that they can't handle simply by trying hard—a great grief, for example. Try hard? You need intake, too. You need sustenance, you need invigoration from beyond yourself.

—Harry Emerson Fosdick

IT IS A fine thing to establish one's own religion in one's heart, not to be dependent on tradition and second-hand ideals. Life will seem to you, later, not a lesser, but a greater thing.

—D. H. Lawrence

DON'T BE AN agnostic. Be *something*.

—Robert Frost

WHATEVER YOU ARE, be a good one.

—Abraham Lincoln

. . . ON SUNDAY GO to church. Yes—I know all the excuses. I know that one can worship the Creator and dedicate oneself to good living in a grove of trees, or by a running brook, or in one's own house, just as well as in church. But I also know that as a matter of cold fact the average man does not thus worship or dedicate himself.

—Theodore Roosevelt

TO LEARN THE worth of a man's religion, do business with him.

—John Lancaster Spalding

Reputation

REGARD YOUR GOOD name as the richest jewel you can possibly be possessed of—for credit is like fire; when once you have kindled it you may easily preserve it, but if you once extinguish it, you will find it an arduous task to rekindle it again. The way to gain a good reputation is to endeavor to be what you desire to appear.

—Socrates

THERE ARE TWO modes of establishing our reputation: to be praised by honest men, and to be abused by rogues. It is best, however, to secure the former, because it will invariably be accompanied by the latter.   —Charles Caleb Colton

HAVE REGARD FOR your name, since it will remain for you longer than a great store of gold.   —Ecclesiasticus, Apocrypha

BETTER BE ILL spoken of by one before all than by all before one.
—Scottish proverb

Resignation/Acceptance

LEARN TO BE pleased with everything; with wealth, so far as it makes us beneficial to others; with poverty, for not having much to care for, and with obscurity, for being unenvied.   —Plutarch

DEMAND NOT THAT events should happen as you wish, but wish them to happen as they do, and you will go on well.   —Epictetus

IF YOU CANNOT catch a bird of paradise, better take a wet hen.
—Nikita Khrushchev

SINCE WE CANNOT get what we like, let us like what we can get.
—Spanish proverb

LET US TAKE things as we find them: let us not attempt to distort them into what they are not. . . . We cannot make facts. All our wishing cannot change them. We must use them.   —John Henry Cardinal Newman

LIVING APART AND at peace with myself, I came to realize more vividly the meaning of the doctrine of acceptance. To refrain from giving advice, to refrain from meddling in the affairs of others, to refrain, even though the motives be the highest, from tampering with another's way of life—so simple, yet so difficult for an active spirit! Hands off!　　　　　　　　　　　　　　　　　　—Henry Miller

ADAPT OR PERISH, now as ever, is nature's inexorable imperative.—H. G. Wells

WHEN DEFEAT IS inevitable, it is wisest to yield.　　—Marcus Fabius Quintilianus

SINCE THE HOUSE is on fire let us warm ourselves.　　　　　—Italian proverb

Resolution

NEVER GIVE IN! Never, never, never, never, never, never. In nothing great or small, large or petty—never give in except to convictions of honor and good sense.　　　　　　　　　　　　　　　　　　　　—Winston Churchill

YOU MAY BE whatever you resolve to be. Determine to be something in the world, and you will be something. "I cannot" never accomplished anything; "I will try" has wrought wonders.　　　　　　　　　　　　　—Joel Hawes

HAVE THE COURAGE of your desire.　　　　　　　　　—George Gissing

WORK AND STRUGGLE and never accept an evil that you can change.　　　　　　　　　　　　　　　　　　　　　　　—André Gide

Rest/Relaxation

IN THE NAME of God, stop a moment, cease your work, look around you . . .
—Leo Tolstoy

TAKE REST; A field that has rested gives a bountiful crop.　　　—Ovid

FIND OUT FOR yourself the form of rest that refreshes you best.
—Daniel Considine

ONE OUGHT, EVERY day at least, to hear a little song, read a good poem, see a fine picture, and, if it were possible, to speak a few reasonable words.—Goethe

WHEN I HAVE nothing to do for an hour, and I don't want to do anything, I neither read nor watch television. I sit back in a chair and let my mind relax. I do what I call idling. It's as if the motorcar's running but you haven't got it in gear. You have to allow a certain amount of time in which you are doing nothing in order to have things occur to you, to let your mind think.　　　—Mortimer Adler

SIT IN REVERIE, and watch the changing color of the waves that break upon the idle seashore of the mind.　　　—Henry Wadsworth Longfellow

FOR FAST-ACTING relief, try slowing down.　　　—Lily Tomlin

NEVER DO ANYTHING standing that you can do sitting, or anything sitting that you can do lying down.　　　—Chinese proverb

EMPLOY THY TIME well, if thou meanest to get leisure.　　　—Benjamin Franklin

LEARN RELAXATION TECHNIQUES: These include deep breathing exercises, transcendental meditation, the "relaxation response" (a demystified form of meditation formulated by Dr. Herbert Benson, a Harvard cardiologist), yoga, progressive relaxation of muscle groups, imagery, biofeedback and behavioral modification. The last four may require professional help. On a tightly scheduled day, take a minute or two between appointments or activities for a relaxation break—stretching, breathing, walking about.

—Jane E. Brody

THERE IS ONE piece of advice, in a life of study, which I think no one will object to; and that is, every now and then to be completely idle—to do nothing at all.

—Sydney Smith

(*See also* Pleasure and Recreation.)

Restraint

NEVER DRAW YOUR dirk when a blow will do it. —Scottish proverb

BE WISER THAN other people if you can; but do not tell them so.
—Lord Chesterfield

DON'T MAKE USE of another's mouth unless it has been lent to you.
—Belgian proverb

USE SOFT WORDS and hard arguments. —English proverb

SUBDUE YOUR APPETITES, my dears, and you've conquered human nature.
—Charles Dickens

Retirement

DON'T SIMPLY RETIRE from something; have something to retire to.
—Harry Emerson Fosdick

BEFORE YOU THINK of retiring from the world, be sure you are fit for retirement; in order to which it is necessary that you have a mind so composed by prudence, reason, and religion, that it may bear being looked into; a turn to rural life, and a love for study. —James Burgh

KNOW WHEN YOUR time is over. It's the only advice I have. Hell, I knew twenty-five years ago it wasn't going to last. Sooner or later, the demand won't be there, and you better get ready for it. I know actresses who go ape if they're not invited to a party. What the hell is that? I am content. Happiness is within yourself. Get ready for the dream to fade. So I'm no longer in demand, but so what? I see no reason to go into a decline or hit the bottle or sink into a melancholy depression. I've had my time and it was lovely. And I'm very grateful for it. But now I move over and make room for somebody else. . . . What the hell. Whatever I had, it worked, didn't it? —Barbara Stanwyck

DON'T THINK OF retiring from the world until the world will be sorry that you retire. I hate a fellow whom pride or cowardice or laziness drives into a corner, and who does nothing when he is there but sit and growl. Let him come out as I do, and bark. —Samuel Johnson

ON RETIREMENT: MY advice is: If at all possible, don't cut your bridges to what you've done and where you've been. —Lucille T. Wessmann

Retribution

> And if any mischief follow, then thou
> shalt give life for life,
>   Eye for eye, tooth for tooth, hand
> for hand, foot for foot,
>   Burning for burning, wound for
> wound, stripe for stripe.
>
> —Old Testament

> Heat not a furnace for your foe so hot
> That it do singe yourself: we may outrun,

By violent swiftness, that which we run at,
And lose by over-running.

—Duke of Norfolk, in Shakespeare's
The Life of King Henry VIII

He for himself weaves woe who weaves for others woe,
And evil counsel on the counselor recoils.

—Hesiod

Revenge

VENGEANCE IS MINE; I will repay, saith the Lord.
Therefore if thine enemy hunger, feed him; if he thirst, give him drink: for in so doing thou shalt heap coals of fire on his head.　　　—New Testament

IN TAKING REVENGE, a man is but even with his enemy; but in passing it over, he is superior.　　　—Francis Bacon

IT IS FOLLY to punish your neighbor by fire when you live next door.

—Publilius Syrus

LIVE WELL. IT is the greatest revenge.　　　—The Talmud

"REJOICE NOT AT thine enemy's fall"—but don't rush to pick him up either.

—Jewish proverb

Riches

Abundance is a blessing to the wise;
The use of riches in discretion lies;
Learn this, ye men of wealth—a heavy purse
In a fool's pocket is a heavy curse.

—Richard Cumberland

LET US NOT envy some men their accumulated riches; their burden would be too heavy for us; we could not sacrifice, as they do, health, quiet, honor and conscience, to obtain them: it is to pay so dear for them that the bargain is a loss.

—Jean de La Bruyère

PEOPLE SAY THAT luxury and comfort and money are bad for the soul. I don't believe it. Nothing is better for the soul than having what you want, and anybody who can become rich and comfortable and doesn't is a damned fool. My uncle's advice is sound. One of the best ways to ensure success is to develop expensive tastes, or marry someone who has them. The range of options open to those who succeed is so large as to encompass almost everything: yachts, art, clothes, jewelry, travel—all these can be yours.

—Michael Korda

IF YOU AREN'T rich, you should always look useful.   —Louis-Ferdinand Céline

IF YOU WOULD be wealthy, think of saving as well as getting.

—Benjamin Franklin

IT REQUIRES A great deal of boldness and a great deal of caution to make a great fortune; and when you have got it, it requires ten times as much wit to keep it.
—Meyer A. Rothschild

BE NOT PENNY-WISE: riches have wings, and sometimes they fly away of themselves; sometimes they must be set flying to bring in more.

BELIEVE NOT MUCH them that seem to despise riches, for they despise them that despair of them.
—Francis Bacon

BE RICH TO yourself and poor to your friends.
—Juvenal

THE BEST WAY to realize the pleasure of feeling rich is to live in a smaller house than your means would entitle you to have.
—Edward Clarke

HE IS NOT fit for riches who is afraid to use them.
—Thomas Fuller

DON'T TRY TO die rich but live rich.
—Thomas Bird Mosher

IN SHORT, PUT your shoulder to the wheel, but be careful to pick the right wheel. Says Sophie Tucker, "I've been rich and I've been poor. Believe me, honey, rich is best."
—David M. Ogilvy

DECEIVE THE RICH and powerful if you will, but don't insult them.
—Japanese proverb

Rightness

NEITHER LET MISTAKES nor wrong directions, of which every man, in his studies and elsewhere, falls into many, discourage you. There is precious instruction to be got by finding we were wrong. Let a man try faithfully, manfully, to be right; he will grow daily more and more right. —Thomas Carlyle

LET US HAVE faith that right makes might; and in that faith let us to the end dare to do our duty as we understand it. —Abraham Lincoln

WHEN YOU ARE right you cannot be too radical; when you are wrong, you cannot be too conservative. —Dr. Martin Luther King, Jr.

DO WHAT YOU feel in your heart to be right—for you'll be criticized anyway. You'll be damned if you do, and damned if you don't. —Eleanor Roosevelt

(*See also* Mistakes.)

Rights

NEVER YIELD YOUR courage—your courage to live, your courage to fight, to resist, to develop your own lives, to be free. I'm talking about resistance to wrong and fighting oppression. —Roger Baldwin

WE SHOULD BE eternally vigilant against attempts to check the expression of opinions that we loathe. —Oliver Wendell Holmes, Jr.

IF YOU WANT to be free, there is but one way; it is to guarantee an equally full measure of liberty to all your neighbors. There is no other. —Carl Schurz

ECRASEZ L'INFÂME. (Wipe out the infamous.)   —Voltaire's motto

IF WE CANNOT secure all our rights, let us secure what we can.

—Thomas Jefferson

Risk

FIRST WEIGH THE considerations, then take the risks.   —Helmuth von Moltke

TAKE CALCULATED RISKS. That is quite different from being rash.

—George S. Patton

RISK! RISK ANYTHING! Care no more for the opinion of others, for those voices. Do the hardest thing on earth for you. Act for yourself. Face the truth.

—Katherine Mansfield

TO DO ANYTHING in this world worth doing, we must not stand back shivering and thinking of the cold and danger, but jump in, and scramble through as well as we can.

—Sydney Smith

Science

REMEMBER THAT SCIENCE claims a man's whole life. Had he two lives they would not suffice. Science demands an undivided allegiance from its followers. In your work and in your research there must always be passion. —Ivan Pavlov

IT IS NOT enough that you should understand about applied science in order that your work may increase man's blessings. Concern for man himself and his fate must always form the chief interest of all technical endeavors, concern for the great unsolved problems of the organization of labor and the distribution of goods—in order that the creations of our mind shall be a blessing and not a curse to mankind. Never forget this in the midst of your diagrams and equations.

—Albert Einstein

PAY CLOSE ATTENTION to . . . tiny chips of silicon that engineers call "integrated circuits." Like the industrial revolution that extended the influence of man's muscles, the electronics revolution will extend the influence of his mind, enabling him to reach new levels of mastery and control. . . . The revolution is spreading through our society. Many of you can contribute directly to the new technology. . . . I urge you to be bold and imaginative. Replace the old with the new when circumstances so dictate. Think in unconventional ways. Create uses never before possible. Invent completely original technologies.

—Harry J. Gray

Secrets

IF YOU WANT to preserve your secret, wrap it up in frankness.

—Michel de Montaigne

IF YOU REVEAL your secrets to the wind you should not blame the wind for revealing them to the trees. —Kahlil Gibran

IMPART TO NONE what you would not have all know. For men are moved to tattle by various motives—some through folly, some for gain, some from an empty desire to be thought knowing. —Francesco Guicciardini

YOUR FRIEND HAS a friend; don't tell him. —Jewish proverb

WOULD YOU KNOW secrets? Look for them in grief or pleasure.—Thomas Fuller

Self

DO NOT SPEAK for other men; speak for yourself. —Henry David Thoreau

DON'T DISCUSS YOURSELF, for you are bound to lose; if you belittle yourself, you are believed; if you praise yourself, you are disbelieved.—Michel de Montaigne

DRAW FROM OTHERS the lesson that may profit yourself. —Terence

DON'T ASK OF your friends what you yourself can do. —Quintus Ennius

Self-Control

CONQUER THYSELF. TILL thou has done this, thou art but a slave; for it is almost as well to be subjected to another's appetite as to thine own.

—Sir Richard Francis Burton

THE SECRET OF all success is to know how to deny yourself. Prove that you can control yourself, and you are an educated man; and without this all other education is good for nothing. —R. D. Hitchcock

EDUCATE YOUR CHILDREN to self-control, to the habit of holding passion and prejudice and evil tendencies subject to an upright and reasoning will, and you have done much to abolish misery from their future lives and crimes from society. —Daniel Webster

Self-Defense

DEFENSE AGAINST MUGGERS: Try not to panic. Do the best you can under a difficult situation. Above all, don't try to be a hero. —Captain E. F. Leija, Houston Police Department

DO NOT RESIST. Immediately hand over your wallet, your watch, your jewelry and anything else the mugger wants. . . . Do not attempt to negotiate for your belongings; the longer you delay the mugger the more impatient, and violent, he is likely to become. If you are held up in an isolated area, do not scream. Chances are that no one will hear your cries for help, and they will only enrage —or perhaps even worse, frighten—the mugger. —*Time* magazine

NEVER GIVE AN armed robber the excuse he is looking for to work you over.

—Detective R. Southerland,
Dade County

Self-Esteem

ABOVE ALL THINGS, reverence yourself.

—Pythagoras

THE WORLD IS as good as you are. You've got to learn to like yourself first. I'm a little screwed up, but I'm beautiful.

—Steve McQueen

IF YOU WANT to be respected, you must respect yourself.

—Spanish proverb

IF YOU REALLY do put a small value upon yourself, rest assured that the world will not raise your price.

—Anonymous

DOUBT WHOM YOU will, but never yourself.

—Christine Bovee

Self-Knowledge

KNOW THEN THYSELF, presume not God to scan;
The proper study of mankind is man.

—Alexander Pope

''KNOW THYSELF'' MEANS this, that you get acquainted with what you know, and what you can do.

—Menander of Athens

KNOW THYSELF. ULYSSES showed his wisdom in not trusting himself. A Yale undergraduate left on his door a placard for the janitor on which was written, "Call me at seven o'clock; it's absolutely necessary that I get up at seven. Make

no mistake. Keep knocking until I answer." Under this he had written, "Try again at ten."
—William Lyon Phelps

BEWARE OF NO Man more than thy self.
—Thomas Fuller

ONLY AS YOU do know yourself can your brain serve you as a sharp and efficient tool. Know your own failings, passions, and prejudices so you can separate them from what you see. Know also when you actually have thought through to the nature of the thing with which you are dealing and when you are not thinking at all.
—Bernard M. Baruch

IF A PERSON is to get the meaning of life he must learn to like the facts about himself—ugly as they may seem to his sentimental vanity—before he can learn the truth behind the facts. And the truth is never ugly.
—Eugene O'Neill

NEVER LOSE SIGHT of this important truth, that no one can be truly great until he has gained a knowledge of himself, a knowledge which can only be acquired by occasional retirement.
—Johann Georg von Zimmermann

EVERYTHING STARTS WITH yourself—with you making up your mind about what you're going to do with your life. I tell kids that it's a cruel world, and that the world will bend them either left or right, and it's up to them to decide which way to bend.
—Tony Dorsett

Self-Reliance

TRUST THYSELF: EVERY heart vibrates to that inner string.

—Ralph Waldo Emerson

USE WHAT TALENTS you possess: the woods would be very silent if no birds sang there except those that sang best. —Henry Van Dyke

A HUMAN BEING is only interesting if he's in contact with himself. I learned you have to trust yourself, be what you are, and do what you ought to do the way you should do it. You have got to discover you, what you do, and trust it.

—Barbra Streisand

AS SOON AS you trust yourself, you will know how to live. —Goethe

YOU CAN LISTEN to what everybody says, but the fact remains that you've got to get out there and do the thing yourself. —Joan Sutherland

> Nothing great is lightly won,
>   Nothing won is lost;
> Every good deed, nobly done,
>   Will repay the cost.
> Leave to Heaven in humble trust,
>   All you will to do;
> But, if you succeed you must
>   Paddle your own canoe.
>
> —Sarah K. Bolton

IF YOU DON'T run your own life, somebody else will. —John Atkinson

RESOLVE TO BE thyself, and know that he
Who finds himself, loses his misery.

—Matthew Arnold

Service To Humanity

I DO WANT to say a few things to the graduates. . . . I ask you to give to your children a better world than we gave to you. I ask you to temper your striving for material success, for the glitter of things, with the drive to overcome the injustice and misery that still stalk our nation and our planet. . . . Be steadfast, be strong, be of good cheer.

—Vernon E. Jordan, Jr.

BE ASHAMED TO die unless you have won some victory for humanity.

—Horace Mann

ONE THING I know: the only ones among you who will be really happy are those who will have sought and found how to serve. . . . Think occasionally of the suffering of which you spare yourself the sight.

—Albert Schweitzer

DEDICATE SOME OF your life to others. Your dedication will not be a sacrifice. It will be an exhilarating experience because it is an intense effort applied toward a meaningful end.

—Dr. Thomas Dooley

SOW GOOD SERVICES; sweet remembrances will grow them.—Madame de Stael

Sex

YOU MUSTN'T FORCE sex to do the work of love or love to do the work of sex.

—Mary McCarthy

TAKE OFF YOUR shell along with your clothes.

—Alex Comfort

ONE THING I'VE learned in all these years is not to make love when you really don't feel it; there's probably nothing worse you can do to yourself than that.

—Norman Mailer

WHEN YOU START planning it and being deliberate about it, it goes wrong. It's usually just when you're both thinking about something else, or rather you're just preoccupied with other people, and boing! That's when it's all right. But you can't make that happen.

—Nelson Algren

WHEN YOU HAVE found the place where a woman loves to be fondled, don't you be ashamed to touch it any more than she is.

—Ovid

DON'T BE FOOLED into believing alcohol is an effective turn-on. A moderate amount reduces the inhibitions—but as Shakespeare said, it increases the desire but damages the performance.

—Ann Landers quoting
Henry W. Brosin, M.D.

THE WOMAN WHO goes to bed with a man should put off her modesty with her skirt and put it on again with her petticoat.

—Michel de Montaigne

IT IS BETTER to be silent than to say things at the wrong time that are too tender; what was appropriate ten seconds ago is so no longer, and hurts one's cause, rather than helps it. —Stendhal

DO NOT RUSH into your own bed after *it*. Talk a little bit, hang around.

—Mel Brooks

ANSWERING QUESTIONS IS a major part of sex education. Two rules cover the ground. First, always give a truthful answer to a question; secondly, regard sex knowledge as exactly like any other knowledge. —Bertrand Russell

HOW TO BE SEXY: Clean hair is sexy. . . . Being able to sit very still is sexy. Smiles are sexy. It is unsexy to talk about members of your family and how cute or awful they are. Or about your boss a lot—he's another man . . . a rival. Talking all the time about anything is unsexy. Sphinxes and Mona Lisas knew what they were doing! Gossip—surprise, surprise—is not unsexy! . . . The little black dress is sexy. . . . Perfume is sexy. Good health is sexy. Liking men is sexy. It is by and large just about the sexiest thing you can do. But I mean really liking, not just pretending. . . . You must spend time plotting how to make him happier. Not just him . . . them! —Helen Gurley Brown

Shopping

YOU CAN'T EAT well and keep fit if you don't shop well. —Adelle Davis

EAT BEFORE SHOPPING. If you go to the store hungry, you are likely to make unnecessary purchases. —*American Heart Association Cookbook*

SHOP EARLY IN the day; the store will not be so crowded, the fresh produce will be fresher, and specials will be readily available.

Shop alone if possible. You will be better able to concentrate, and other members of the family will not be adding unnecessary—and often expensive—items to the shopping cart. —*The Redbook Cookbook*

DON'T BUY THE "special" without checking quality. The apple in that marked-down bag may be bruised. Don't buy food you don't need just because it's cheap. A bargain that turns spoiled is no bargain. Don't buy too far in advance. There's such a thing as over-planning in food buying. Fresh meat, vegetables and fruit all tend to lose flavor even when they're stored in the refrigerator.

—James A. Beard

Simplicity

SIMPLICITY, SIMPLICITY, SIMPLICITY! I say, let your affairs be as two or three, and not a hundred or a thousand; instead of a million count half a dozen, and keep your accounts on your thumbnail. . . . Simplify, simplify.

—Henry David Thoreau

EVERYTHING SHOULD BE made as simple as possible, but not one bit simpler.

—Albert Einstein

WHEN A THOUGHT is too weak to be expressed simply, simply drop it.

—Marquis de Vauvenargues

THE AIM OF science is to seek the simplest explanations of complex facts. We are apt to fall into the error of thinking that the facts are simple because simplicity is the goal of our quest. The guiding motto in the life of every natural philosopher should be, "Seek simplicity and distrust it." —Alfred North Whitehead

Singleness

A SINGLE WOMAN'S life is *not* particularly orderly. You have to take when the taking is good . . . the riotous living when it's offered, the quiet when there's nothing else. . . . You may marry or you may not. In today's world that is no longer the big question for women. . . . You, my friend, if you work at it, can be envied the rich, full life possible for the single woman today. It's a good show . . . enjoy it, from wherever you are, whether it's two in the balcony or one on the aisle—don't miss *any* of it.   —Helen Gurley Brown

GET AWAY FROM the crowd when you can. Keep yourself to yourself, if only for a few hours daily.   —Arthur Brisbane

ALONE IS A good way to go to a fight or the races, because you have more time to look around you, and you can always get all the conversation you can use anyway.   —A. J. Liebling

Skepticism

LOVE YOUR NEIGHBOR, but don't tear down the fence.   —German proverb

CALL NO MAN foe, but never love a stranger.   —Stella Benson

NEVER TRUST A man who speaks well of everybody.   —John Churton Collins

LET US HAVE a care not to disclose our hearts to those who shut up theirs against us.   —Francis Beaumont

MISTRUST THE MAN who finds everything good, the man who finds everything evil and still more the man who is indifferent to everything. —Johann K. Lavater

DO NOT TRUST the man who tells you all his troubles but keeps from you his joys.   —Jewish proverb

ONE'S FIRST STEP in wisdom is to question everything—and one's last is to come to terms with everything.   —Georg Christoph Lichtenberg

Slander

NEVER TELL EVIL of a man, if you do not know it for a certainty, and if you know it for a certainty, then ask yourself, "Why should I tell it?"
—Johann K. Lavater

TO PERSEVERE IN one's duty and be silent, is the best answer to calumny.
—George Washington

HAVE PATIENCE AWHILE; slanders are not long-lived. Truth is the child of time; ere long she shall appear to vindicate thee.   —Immanuel Kant

BELIEVE NOTHING AGAINST another but on good authority; and never report what may hurt another, unless it be a greater hurt to some other to conceal it.
—William Penn

THE MAN WHO backbites an absent friend, nay, who does not stand up for him when another blames him, the man who angles for bursts of laughter and for the repute of a wit, who can invent what he never saw, who cannot keep a secret— that man is black at heart: mark and avoid him, if you are a Roman.   —Cicero

Sleeping/Waking

IN THE MORNING be first up, and in the evening last to go to bed, for they that sleep catch no fish.
—English proverb

LET YOUR SLEEP be necessary and healthful, not idle and expensive of time beyond the needs and conveniences of nature; and sometimes be curious to see the preparation the sun makes when he is coming forth from his chambers in the east.
—Jeremy Taylor

IF YOU CAN'T sleep, then get up and do something instead of lying there and worrying. It's the worry that gets you, not the loss of sleep.
—Dale Carnegie

BETTER TO GET up late and be wide awake than to get up early and be asleep all day.
—Anonymous

PUT OFF THY cares with thy clothes; so shall thy rest strengthen thy labor, and so thy labor sweeten thy rest.
—Francis Quarles

DON'T GO TO bed too full or too hungry. . . . Cut down on cigarettes and caffeine. These stimulants can jangle your nerves for hours into the night. . . . Turn yourself down toward the end of the day. Put duties aside at least an hour before bed and perform soothing, quiet activities that will help you relax.

DEVELOP A SLEEP ritual. This may be as simple as lying in bed and listening to soft music for a few minutes. . . . Avoid naps. The more you sleep by day, the more inefficiently you sleep at night. And the longer the nap, the greater the impact it may have on your nighttime rest.
—Dianne Hales

EXERCISE MILDLY TWO hours before bedtime. A few situps or a ten-minute walk may relax your body for sleep. Anything strenuous, like running, is too stimulating. Avoid exercising just before bedtime. . . . Go to bed earlier if you feel and look tired. . . . Throw out an alarming alarm clock. If the ring is loud and strident, you're waking up to instant stress. You shouldn't be bullied out of bed, just reminded that it's time to start your day.　　—Sharon Gold

Smoking

A MAN DOES not have to light a woman's cigarette in the evening or at any time. Since smoking is a death warrant for some people, it is no longer considered good manners to help someone sign that warrant.　　—Letitia Baldrige

HERE . . . IS why you should not smoke. Smoking cigarettes is likely to shorten your life. . . . Smoking directly causes or contributes to the three main causes of American deaths: heart disease, cancer and accidents.

THOUGH MANY SMOKERS justify the continuation of their habit on the ground that it is too late to quit because the damage has already been done, the facts show otherwise. Ten to fifteen years after stopping smoking, your risk of dying prematurely comes close to that of those who have never smoked. Although those who quit before age forty benefit most, the risk of death and disability from smoking declines at any point that you quit. . . . In addition there are immediate benefits of quitting: a decline in the oxygen-robbing carbon monoxide in the blood, improved sleep, the disappearance of headaches and stomachaches caused by smoking, enhanced stamina, keener senses of taste and smell and, after a few years, the disappearance of smoker's cough.　　—Jane E. Brody

REMOVE A CIGAR from your mouth if you meet a lady.　　—C. B. Hartley, 1873

Solitude

IN WHAT CONCERNS you much, do not think that you have companions: know that you are alone in the world.

—Henry David Thoreau

WHEN YOU HAVE shut your doors, and darkened your room, remember, never to say that you are alone, for you are not alone, but God is within, and your genius is within.

—Epictetus

YOU DO NOT need to leave your room. Remain sitting at your table and listen. Do not even listen, simply wait. Do not even wait, be quite still and solitary. The world will freely offer itself to you to be unmasked, it has no choice, it will roll in ecstasy at your feet.

—Franz Kafka

Speaking

FIRST LEARN THE meaning of what you say, and then speak.

—Epictetus

> Speak clearly, if you speak at all;
> Carve every word before you let it fall.
>
> —Oliver Wendell Holmes, Jr.

YOU MAY USE different sorts of sentences and illustrations before different sorts of audiences, but you don't—if you are wise—talk down to any audience.

—Norman Thomas

> Speak boldly, and speak truly.
> Shame the devil.
>
> —John Fletcher

CONSULT A DICTIONARY for proper meanings and pronunciations. Your audience won't know if you're a bad speller, but they will know if you use or pronounce a word improperly. In my first remarks on the dais, I used to thank people for their "fulsome introduction," until I discovered to my dismay that "fulsome" means offensive and insincere.

—George Plimpton

(*See also* Oratory and Public Speaking.)

Speculation

REMEMBER, MY SON, that any man who is a bear on the future of this country will go broke.
—John Pierpont Morgan

DON'T SPECULATE UNLESS you can make it a full-time job. Beware of barbers, beauticians, waiters—of anyone—bringing gifts of "inside" information or "tips". . . . Don't try to buy at the bottom and sell at the top. This can't be done —except by liars.
—Bernard M. Baruch

NEVER INVEST IN anything that eats or needs repairing.
—Billy Rose

BUY ON THE rumor; sell on the news.
—Wall Street proverb

BEHOLD, THE FOOL sayeth: "Put not all thine eggs in the one basket"—which is but a manner of saying, "Scatter your money and your attention." But the wise man saith, "Put all your eggs in one basket and—WATCH THAT BASKET."
—Mark Twain

YOU MUST LOSE a fly to catch a trout.
—George Herbert

DON'T GAMBLE; TAKE all your savings and buy some good stock and hold it till it goes up, then sell it. If it don't go up, don't buy it.
—Will Rogers

AVOID THE CROWD. Do your own thinking independently. Be the chess player, not the chess piece.
—Ralph Charell

Sports

RUN TO DAYLIGHT.

You've got to be in top physical condition. Fatigue makes cowards of us all.
—Vince Lombardi

TO BECOME A champion, fight one more round.
—James J. Corbett

I THINK [HER defeated opponent] still thinks you can win on talent alone. But you've got to be gutsy, and you've got to play smart . . .

If you can react the same way to winning and losing, that's a big accomplishment. That quality is important because it stays with you the rest of your life, and there's going to be a life after tennis that's a lot longer than your tennis life.
—Chris Evert

IF YOU BREAK 100, watch your golf. If you break 80, watch your business.
—Joey Adams

TIP ON HITTING (BASEBALL): The pitcher has to throw the ball in the strike zone sooner or later and the rules allow the hitter to hit only one fair ball each time he bats, so why not hit the pitch you want to hit and not the one he wants you to hit?
—Johnny Mize

Sports/Teamwork

WHOEVER WANTS TO learn the heart and mind of America had better learn baseball, the rules and realities of the game—and do it by watching first some high school or small town teams.
—Jacques Barzun

I'M JUST A plowhand from Arkansas, but I have learned how to hold a team together. How to lift some men up, how to calm down others, until finally they've got one heartbeat, together, a team. There's just three things I ever say. If anything goes bad, then I did it. If anything goes semi-good, then we did it. If anything goes real good, then you did it. That's all it takes to get people to win football games for you. —Bear Bryant

ONE MAN MAY hit the mark, another blunder; but heed not these distinctions. Only from the alliance of the one, working with and through the other, are great things born. —Antoine de Saint-Exupéry

Stress/Tension

DON'T BE AFRAID to enjoy the stress of a full life nor too naive to think you can do so without some intelligent thinking and planning. Man should not try to avoid stress any more than he would shun food, love, or exercise. . . . Trying to remember too many things is certainly one of the major sources of psychologic stress. I make a conscious effort to forget immediately all that is unimportant and to jot down data of possible value. . . . This technique can help anyone to accomplish the greatest simplicity compatible with the degree of complexity of his intellectual life. —Dr. Hans Selye

DISTRACT YOUR MIND when you're under pressure. Do something frivolous, nonstressful and unrelated to "real life." Watch an old movie on TV, play with your dog, do a crossword puzzle, take a long swim. —Sharon Gold

NO MATTER HOW much pressure you feel at work, if you could find ways to relax for at least five minutes every hour, you'd be more productive. Most stress we bring on ourselves through bad habits and bad attitudes. Take a pencil and paper and write down everything in your day that produces stress, checking the aggravations that create the greatest stress. Analyze all the ways you might change these situations. If you talked with a co-worker, would it ease the stress? If you got up half an hour earlier, could you stop running and take time to walk, or even stroll? Do you exercise at least twenty minutes a day? If you don't, you should, because it will relieve stress and allow you to work and sleep better.

—Dr. Joyce Brothers

REMEMBER WHEN LIFE'S path is steep to keep your mind even.   —Horace

STEPS A PERSON CAN TAKE TO RELIEVE STRESS: Talk it out. When something worries you, don't bottle it up. . . . *Escape for a while.* When things go wrong, it helps to escape from the painful problem for a while. . . . *Work off your anger.* Do something constructive with the pent-up energy. Pitch into some physical activity or work it out in tennis or a long walk. . . . *Do something for others.* If you feel yourself worrying about yourself all the time, try doing something for somebody else. . . . *Take one thing at a time.* Take a few of the most urgent tasks and pitch into them, one at a time; setting aside all the rest for the time being. *Shun the "superman" urge.* No one can be perfect in everything.

—Suggestions from the
National Mental Health Association,
reported by Dr. Neil Solomon

ON COPING WITH THE PRESSURE OF NEW STARDOM: Start with one thing: that they need you. Without you they have an empty screen. So, when you get on there, just do what you think is right and stay with it. From that point on, you're on your own. . . . If you listen to all the clowns around you're just dead. Go do what you have to do.   —James Cagney, advice to John Travolta

Studying

THE MUSES LOVE the Morning, and that is a fit Time for Study. After you have din'd, either divert yourself at some Exercise, or take a Walk, and discourse merrily, and Study between whiles. As for Diet, eat only as much as shall be sufficient to preserve Health, and not as much or more than the Appetite may crave. Before Supper, take a little Walk and do the same after Supper. A little while before you go to sleep read something that is exquisite, and worth remembering; and contemplate upon it till you fall asleep; and when you awake in the Morning, call yourself to an Account for it.

—Erasmus

TO SPEND TOO much Time in Studies, is Sloth; To use them too much for Ornament, is Affectation; To make Judgment wholly by their rules is the humour of a Scholar.

—Francis Bacon

AS TO YOUR method of work . . . take no thought for the morrow. Live neither in the past nor in the future, but let each day's work absorb your entire energies, and satisfy your widest ambition. That was a singular but very wise answer which Cromwell gave to Bellvire—"No one rises so high as he who knows not whither he is going," and there is much truth in it. The student who is worrying about his future, anxious over the examinations, doubting his fitness for the procession, is certain not to do so well as the man who cares for nothing but the matter in hand, and who knows not whither he is going!

—Sir William Osler to his students

SAY NOT, WHEN I have leisure I will study; you may not have leisure.

—The Mishnah

THEREFORE, O STUDENTS, study mathematics and do not build without foundations.
—Leonardo da Vinci

Style

STYLE IS THE dress of thoughts; let them be ever so just, if your style is homely, coarse, and vulgar, they will appear to as much disadvantage, and be as ill received, as your person, though ever so well proportioned, would be if dressed in rags, dirt and tatters.
—Lord Chesterfield

WHATEVER YOU DO, kid, always serve it with a little dressing.
—George M. Cohan, to Spencer Tracy

IF ANY MAN wish to write in a clear style, let him be first clear in his thoughts; and if any would write in a noble style, let him first possess a noble soul.—Goethe

I WOULD RECOMMEND against the adoption of any one style of prose, regardless of what that style might be. We must resist the blandishments of those who argue for the light touch or humor or humility or totally disarming candor. Each style has its place and time but none is right for every place and time. . . . William Faulkner . . . wrote his World War I fiction in staccato sentences. Later, when he was writing the Yoknapatawpha County books, he employed a more languorous style more in keeping with that setting.
—Melvin J. Grayson

WHEN "WHOM" IS correct, use some other formulation.
—William Safire

ELIESMALT] ouSfix*/

Success

ALWAYS BEAR IN mind that your own resolution to succeed is more important than any one thing.
—Abraham Lincoln

TRY NOT TO become a man of success but rather to become a man of value
—Albert Einstein

FOR ANY WOMAN to succeed in American life she must first do two things: Prepare herself for a profession, and marry a man who wants her to succeed as much as she does.
—Cathleen (Mrs. William O.) Douglas

THE SECRET OF success is constancy to purpose.
—Benjamin Disraeli

MAKING A SUCCESS of the job at hand is the best step toward the kind you want.
—Bernard M. Baruch

DO YOU WISH to become rich? You may become so if you desire it in no half-way, but thoroughly. Do you wish to master any science or accomplishment? Give yourself to it and it lies beneath your feet. This world is given as the prize for the men in earnest; and that which is true of this world, is truer still of the world to come.
—Frederick William Robertson

IF YOU WISH success in life, make perseverance your bosom friend, experience your wise counselor, caution your elder brother and hope your guardian genius.
—Joseph Addison

I CAN GIVE you a six-word formula for success: "Think things through—then follow through."
—Edward Vernon (Eddie) Rickenbacker

335

S

THE TOUGHEST THING about success is that you've got to keep on being a success. Talent is only a starting point in this business. You've got to keep on working that talent. Someday I'll reach for it and it won't be there.—Irving Berlin

I CAN'T GIVE you a sure-fire formula for success, but I can give you a formula for failure: try to please everybody all the time.   —Herbert Bayard Swope

CULTIVATE YOUR CURIOSITY. Keep it sharp and always working. Consider curiosity your life preserver, your willingness to try something new. Second, *enlarge your enthusiasm* to include the pursuit of excellence, following every task through to completion. Third, *make the law of averages work for you.* By budgeting your time more carefully than most people you can make more time available. . . . Does the combination of curiosity, enthusiasm and the law of averages guarantee success? Indeed it does not! . . . Success in the final analysis always involves luck or the element of chance. Louis Pasteur grasped this well when he said that chance favors the prepared mind.   —John W. Hanley

SUCCESS IS A . . . trendy word. Don't aim for success if you want it; just do what you love and it will come naturally.   —David Frost

I BELIEVE THE true road to preeminent success in any line is to make yourself master of that line.   —Andrew Carnegie

A GREAT SECRET of success is to go through life as a man who never gets used up.   —Albert Schweitzer

TO FOLLOW, WITHOUT halt, one aim: There's the secret of success.

—Anna Pavlova

NEVER CONTINUE IN a job you don't enjoy. If you're happy in what you're doing, you'll like yourself, you'll have inner peace. And if you have that, along with physical health, you will have had more success than you could possibly have imagined.

—Johnny Carson

Suffering

Know how sublime it is
To suffer and be strong.

—Henry Wadsworth Longfellow

FORGET YOUR PERSONAL tragedy. We are all bitched from the start and you especially have to be hurt like hell before you can write seriously. But when you get the damned hurt use it—don't cheat with it.

—Ernest Hemingway, in a letter to F. Scott Fitzgerald

THE TRUTH THAT many people never understand, until it is too late, is that the more you try to avoid suffering the more you suffer because smaller and more insignificant things begin to torture you in proportion to your fear of being hurt.

—Thomas Merton

YOU DESIRE TO know the art of living, my friend?
It is contained in one phrase: make use of suffering.

—Henri F. Amiel

Sympathy

LEARN TO MAKE yourself akin to people. . . . But let this sympathy be not with the mind—for it is easy with the mind—but with the heart, with love towards them.

—Unattributed, quoted by Virginia Woolf

REJOICE WITH THEM that do rejoice, and weep with them that weep.

—New Testament

IF YOU WISH me to weep, you must mourn first yourself. —Horace

OPEN YOUR EYES and look for some man, or some work for the sake of men, which needs a little time, a little friendship, a little sympathy, a little sociability, a little human toil. . . . Who can reckon up all the ways in which that priceless fund of impulse, man, is capable of exploitation! He is needed in every nook and corner. Therefore search and see if there is not some place where you may invest your humanity. —Albert Schweitzer

TACT · TALENT · TEMPTATION · THEATER/ACTING/COMEDY · THOUGHT

TIME · TIMELINESS · TOLERANCE · TRADITION · TRAVEL · TROUBLE · TRUST

Tact

DON'T FLATTER YOURSELF that friendship authorizes you to say disagreeable things to your intimates. The nearer you come into relation with a person, the more necessary do tact and courtesy become. Except in cases of necessity, which are rare, leave your friend to learn unpleasant things from his enemies; they are ready enough to tell them. —Oliver Wendell Holmes

> If your lips would keep from slips,
>   Five things observe with care;
> To whom you speak, of whom you speak,
>   And how, and when, and where.
>
> —W. E. Norris

NEVER TELL A man you can read him through and through; most people prefer to be thought enigmas. —Marchioness Townsend

YOU NEVER KNOW till you try to reach them how accessible men are; but you must approach each man by the right door. —Henry Ward Beecher

IT IS NOT enough to do good; one must do it the right way.
—John, Viscount Morley, of Blackburn

DO NOT SPEAK of your happiness to one less fortunate than yourself.—Plutarch

DECEIVE THE RICH and powerful if you will, but don't insult them.
—Japanese proverb

LET YOUR WIT rather serve you for a buckler to defend yourself, by a handsome reply, than the sword to wound others, though with never so facetious approach, remembering that a word cuts deeper than a sharper weapon, and the wound it makes is longer in curing.　　—Francis Osborn, advice to his son, 1656

(*See also* Courtesy/Propriety.)

Talent

TOIL TO MAKE yourself remarkable by some talent or other.　　—Seneca

WHATEVER YOU ARE by nature, keep to it; never desert your line of talent. Be what nature intended you for and you will succeed.　　—Sydney Smith

IF YOU HAVE a talent, use it in every which way possible. Don't hoard it. Don't dole it out like a miser. Spend it lavishly like a millionaire intent on going broke.
　　—Brendan Francis

Hide not your talents, they for use were made.
What's a Sun-dial in the Shade?

　　—Benjamin Franklin

PUT YOURSELF ON view. This brings your talents to light.

　　—Baltasar Gracian

WORK WHILE YOU have the light. You are responsible for the talent that has been entrusted to you.　　—Henri F. Amiel

Temptation

LUST NOT AFTER her beauty in thine heart; neither let her take thee with her eyelids.
—Old Testament, Proverbs

DO NOT LOOK too long on the beauty that belongs to someone else.
—Ecclesiasticus

BETTER SHUN THE bait, than struggle in the snare.
—John Dryden

DO NOT GIVE dalliance too much the rein: the strongest oaths are straw to th' fire i' th' blood.
—Prospero, in Shakespeare's
The Tempest

Theater/Acting/Comedy

IF YOU WANT something from an audience, you give blood to their fantasies. It's the *ultimate* hustle.
—Marlon Brando

TO "METHOD" ACTORS: Speak clearly, don't bump into people, and if you must have motivation think of your pay packet on Friday. . . .

To playwrights: Consider the public. Treat it with tact and courtesy. It will accept much from you if you are clever enough to win it to your side. Never fear it or despise it. Coax it, charm it, interest it, stimulate it, shock it now and then if you must, make it laugh, make it cry, but above all, dear pioneers . . . never, never, never, bore the living hell out of it.
—Sir Noel Coward

HAVE PATIENCE WITH the jealousies and petulances of actors, for their hour is their eternity.
—Richard Garnett

MAKE FRIENDS WITH yourself and then make friends with people. The public has to relate to what you do. Comics today do a small comedy bit but can't follow through. They don't know how to develop it. They're afraid to stand up there for more than two minutes. You've got to stand there and work.—Sid Caesar

Thought

REAL, CONSTRUCTIVE MENTAL power lies in the creative thought that shapes your destiny, and your hour-by-hour mental conduct produces power for change in your life. Develop a train of thought on which to ride. The nobility of your life as well as your happiness depends upon the direction in which that train of thought is going.
—Laurence J. Peter

Men of thought, be up and stirring
Night and day;
Sew and seed—withdraw the curtain—
Clear the way.

—Charles Mackay

FOLLOW THE PATH of the unsafe, independent thinker. Expose your ideas to the dangers of controversy. Speak your mind and fear less the label of "crackpot" than the stigma of conformity. And on issues that seem important to you, stand up and be counted at any cost.
—Thomas J. Watson

THINK TODAY, AND speak tomorrow.
—H. C. Bohn

LET NO MAN imagine that he has no influence. Whoever he may be, and wherever he may be placed, *the man who thinks* becomes a light and a power.

—Henry George

THINK LIKE A man of action, act like a man of thought.   —Henri Bergson

YOU MAY DERIVE thoughts from others; your way of thinking, the mould in which your thoughts are cast, must be your own.   —Charles Lamb

DIVE INTO THE sea of thought, and find there pearls beyond price.

—Moses Ibn Ezra, Shirat Yisrael

MAN IS BUT a reed, the most feeble thing in nature; but he is a thinking reed. The entire universe need not arm itself to crush him. A vapour, a drop of water suffices to kill him. But, if the universe were to crush him, man would still be more noble than that which killed him, because he knows that he dies and the advantage which the universe has over him; the universe knows nothing of this.

All our dignity consists then, in thought. By it we must elevate ourselves, and not by space and time which we cannot fill. Let us endeavor, then, to think well; this is the principle of morality.   —Blaise Pascal

NURTURE YOUR MIND with great thoughts; to believe in the heroic makes heroes.   —Benjamin Disraeli

ALWAYS AIM AT complete harmony of thought and word and deed. Always aim at purifying your thoughts and everything will be well. There is nothing more potent than thought. Deed follows word and word follows thought. The word is the result of a mighty thought, and where the thought is mighty and pure the result is always mighty and pure.   —Mohandas K. Gandhi

Time

Gather ye rosebuds while ye may,
Old Time is still a-flying;
And this same flower that smiles to-day
To-morrow will be dying.

—Robert Herrick

TIME IS THE coin of your life. It is the only coin you have, and only you can determine how it will be spent. Be careful lest you let other people spend it for you.
—Carl Sandburg

GO, SIR, GALLOP, and do not forget that the world took only six days for creation. Ask me for whatever you please, except time; that is the only thing which is beyond my power.
—Napoleon Bonaparte

Come, fill the cup, and in the fire of spring
Your winter garment of repentance fling:
The bird of time has but a little way
To flutter—and the bird is on the wing.

—Omar Khayyam

ONE CAN ALWAYS trust to time; insert a wedge of time, and nearly everything straightens itself out.
—Norman Douglas

Timeliness

If you trap the moment before it's ripe,
The tears of repentance you'll certainly wipe;
But if once you let the right moment go
You can never wipe off the tears of woe.

—William Blake

MISS NOT THE occasion; by the forelock take that subtle power, the never-halting time.

—William Wordsworth

WHY NOT SEIZE the pleasure at once? How often is happiness destroyed by preparation, foolish preparation!

—Jane Austen

BETTER THREE HOURS too soon than a minute too late.

—Ford, in Shakespeare's
The Merry Wives of Windsor

Tolerance

TREAT THE OTHER man's faith gently; it is all he has to believe with. His mind was created for his own thoughts, not yours or mine. —Henry S. Haskins

LEAVE EACH ONE his touch of folly; it helps to lighten life's burden which, if he could see himself as he is, might be too heavy to carry.—John Lancaster Spalding

GIVE TO EVERY other human being every right that you claim for yourself. —Robert G. Ingersoll

LIVE AND LET live. —Johann von Schiller

BE ENTIRELY TOLERANT or not at all; follow the good path or the evil one. To stand at the crossroads requires more strength than you possess.—Heinrich Heine

Tradition

BE NOT SO bigoted to any custom as to worship it at the expense of truth. —Johann Georg von Zimmermann

WE LIVE IN a time of transition, an uneasy era which is likely to endure for the rest of this century. . . . During the period we may be tempted to abandon some of the time-honored principles and commitments which have been proven during the difficult times of past generations. We must never yield to this temptation. Our American values are not luxuries, but necessities—not the salt in our bread but the bread itself. —Jimmy Carter, in his farewell address

REMOVE NOT THE ancient landmark, which the fathers have set. —Old Testament, Proverbs

Travel

TRAVEL IN THE younger sort, is a part of education, in the elder a part of experience. . . . Let him carry with him. . . . some card or book describing the country where he traveleth; which will be a good key to his inquiry. Let him keep also a diary. Let him not stay long in one city or town; more or less as the place deserveth, but not long; nay, when he stayeth in one city or town, let him change his lodging from one end and part of the town to another; which is the great adamant of acquaintance. Let him sequester himself from the company of his countrymen, and diet in such places where there is good company of the nation where he traveleth. Let him also see and visit eminent persons in all kinds, which are of great name abroad; that he may be able to tell how the life agreeth with the fame. . . . When a traveler returneth home, let him not leave the countries where he has traveled altogether behind him, but maintain a correspondence by letters with those of his acquaintance which are of most worth.

—Francis Bacon

ROAM ABROAD IN the world, and take thy fill of its enjoyments before the day shall come when thou must quit it for good. —Saadi

IF YOU REJECT the food, ignore the customs, fear the religion and avoid the people, you might better stay home. You are like a pebble thrown into water; you become wet on the surface but you are never part of the water.

—James A. Michener

OWN ONLY WHAT you can carry with you; know language, know countries, know people. Let your memory be your travel bag.　—Alexander Solzhenitsyn

HE WHO WOULD travel happily must travel light.　—Antoine de Saint-Exupéry

TO DRINK IN the spirit of a place you should be not only alone but not hurried.

—George Santayana

WHEN YOU TRAVEL, remember that a foreign country is not designed to make you comfortable. It is designed to make its own people comfortable.

—Clifton Fadiman

TRAVEL ONLY WITH thy equals or thy betters; if there are none, travel alone.

—The Dhammapada

Turn all care out of your head as soon as
you mount the chaise.

Do not think about frugality; your health is
worth more than it can cost.

Do not continue any day's journey to fatigue.

Take now and then a day's rest.

Cast away all anxiety, and keep your mind
easy.

—Samuel Johnson

AVOID PLAYS ACTED in a foreign language, and buildings entirely rebuilt since the war. Beware of government-sponsored stores and light operas. Limit yourself to one cathedral, one picture gallery, and one giant Buddha a week.

—Robert Morley

DON'T STAY AT home and putter around the house. You need a change of scene.

Take your wife, but leave the children with a neighbor. Small fry are a pain in the neck on a vacation. . . .

Broaden your horizons by going abroad, even if you have to travel steerage. But don't travel so much that you come back cross and exhausted.

—David M. Ogilvy

WATCH WHAT YOU eat or drink. You should not eat the lettuce; it is fine to eat vegetables that are cooked. When I travel, I often drink beer, rather than water. Beer is usually free of various infectious agents. . . . If you do come back sick, be prepared to tell your physician exactly where you traveled. For instance, not "Southeast Asia," but the name of the country, the province and the town. . . . The only worry about water is of that you drink. It's fine to take showers and wash, as long as the water is not a river in the tropics. . . . If you eat shellfish cooked, you are all right.

—Dr. Allen W. Methies, Jr.
Dean, USC School of Medicine

Trouble

TROUBLE IS PART of your life, and if you don't share it, you don't give the person who loves you a chance to love you enough. —Dinah Shore

IF YOU DON'T learn to laugh at trouble, you won't have anything to laugh at when you're old.

—Ed Howe

MEET THE FIRST beginnings; look to the budding mischief before it has time to ripen to maturity.
—Anonymous

NEVER TROUBLE TROUBLE till trouble troubles you.
—American proverb

Trust

THE CHIEF LESSON I have learned in a long life is that the only way to make a man trustworthy is to trust him; and the surest way to make him untrustworthy is to distrust him and show your distrust.
—Henry L. Stimson

TRUST EVERYBODY, BUT cut the cards.
—Finley Peter Dunne

YOU MAY BE deceived if you trust too much, but you will live in torment if you do not trust enough.
—Frank Crane

Truth

SAY NOT, ''I have found the truth," but rather, "I have found a truth."
—Kahlil Gibran

DO NOT THINK that *your* truth can be found by anyone else; be ashamed of nothing more than of that.
—André Gide

TELL THE TRUTH, and so puzzle and confound your adversaries.
—Sir Henry Wotton

WHEN IN DOUBT, tell the truth.
—Mark Twain

WHEN THOU ART obliged to speak, be sure to speak the truth, for equivocation is half way to lying, and lying is whole way to hell. —William Penn

LOOK AT ALL the sentences which seem true and question them.

—David Reisman

FIGHT FOR YOUR opinions, but do not believe that they contain the whole truth, or the only truth. —Charles A. Dana

TRUTH IS ALWAYS exciting. Speak it, then. Life is dull without it.—Pearl S. Buck

CHASE AFTER TRUTH like hell and you'll free yourself, even though you never touch its coat-tails. —Clarence Darrow

LET NOT MERCY and truth forsake thee; bind them about thy neck; write them upon the table of thine heart. —Old Testament

WHAT IS IMPORTANT is to keep learning, to enjoy challenge, and to tolerate ambiguity. In the end there are no certain answers. —Martina Horner
President, Radcliffe College

IF YOU ARE out to describe the truth, leave elegance to the tailor.

—Albert Einstein

V

Venerability

Grow old along with me!
The best is yet to be,
The last of life, for which the first was made.

—Robert Browning

AGE TO ME means nothing. I can't get old; I'm working. I was old when I was twenty-one and out of work. As long as you're working, you stay young. When I'm in front of an audience, all that love and vitality sweeps over me and I forget my age.
—George Burns

LET US RESPECT gray hairs, especially our own.
—J. P. Senn

NEVER LOSE SIGHT of the fact that old age needs so little but needs that little so much.
—Margaret Willour

TO RESIST THE frigidity of old age one must combine the body, the mind and the heart—and to keep them in parallel vigor one must exercise, study and love.
—Karl von Bonstetten

I HAVE DISCOVERED the secret formula for a carefree Old Age: ICR—FI—"If You Can't Recall It, Forget It."
—Goodman Ace

DISCERN OF THE coming on of years, and think not to do the same things still, for age will not be denied.
—Francis Bacon

Vice

BEWARE OF THE beginnings of vice. . . . Do not delude yourself with the belief that it can be argued against in the presence of the exciting cause. . . . Nothing but actual flight can save you. —B. R. Haydon

IF YOU WOULD not step into the harlot's house, do not go by the harlot's door.
—Thomas Secker

DO NOT TAKE drugs because they demand periodic doses and your heart will crave them. You will also lose money. Even for medicinal purposes do not take drugs if you can find a different medicine that will help.
—Samuel ben Meir (1085–1158),
commentary on the Talmud

CULTIVATE VICES WHEN you are young, and when you are old they will not forsake you. —Anonymous

NURSE ONE VICE in your bosom. Give it the attention it deserves and let your virtues spring up modestly around it. Then you'll have the miser who's no liar; and the drunkard who's the benefactor of a whole city. —Thornton Wilder

NEVER OPEN THE door to a little vice lest a great one enter with it.—Anonymous

Virtue

I DO NOTHING but go about persuading you all, old and young alike, not to take thought for your persons or your properties, but and chiefly to care about the greatest improvement of the soul. I tell you that virtue is not given by money, but that from virtue comes money and every other good of man, public as well as private. This is my teaching, and if this is the doctrine which corrupts the youth, I am a mischievous person.　　　　—Socrates, in Plato's

The Death of Socrates

RECOMMEND TO YOUR children virtue; that alone can make them happy, not gold.　　　　—Ludwig van Beethoven

SEARCH OTHERS FOR their virtues, thyself for thy vices.　　—Benjamin Franklin

ENJOY YOUR ACHIEVEMENTS as well as your plans. Keep interested in your career, however humble; it is a real possession in the changing fortunes of time. Exercise caution in your business affairs, for the world is full of trickery. But let this not blind you to what virtue there is; many persons strive for high ideals; and everywhere life is full of heroism.　　—Anonymous (found at Adlai Stevenson's

bedside after his death)

Visiting

THE GUEST:

Don't bring your children uninvited.
Leave your pets at home.
Arrive on time, leave on time, never stay over "for just another day."
Don't arrive sick. Cancel. No one likes to run a sick ward for a guest.
Bring a tasteful, useful present—like food or liquor or a great new family game.
Keep your quarters very neat and tidy.
Keep off your host's telephone; when you call long distance, use your credit card or pay back your host immediately.
Be on time, properly dressed, for every part of the schedule.

If you break something, report it and replace it.
Be considerate to all members of the host's family.
Write a warm personal letter of thanks to your hosts after the weekend, mention details of things that pleased you.
If you didn't bring a "hostess present," send one after your return home.

—Letitia Baldrige

YOU MAY LAUGH at a friend's roof; don't laugh at his sleeping accommodation.

—Bondei (Kenya) proverb

BE NOT SLOW to visit the sick.   —Ecclesiastes

WHERESOEVER YOU GO, go with all your heart.   —Confucian proverb

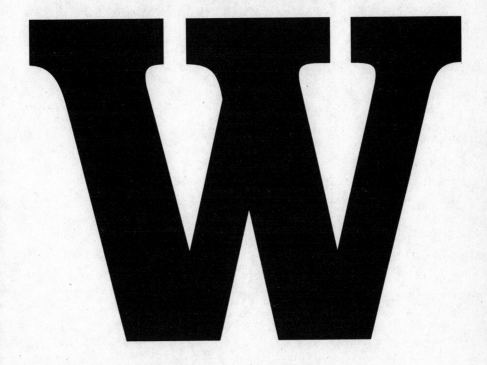

WALKING   •   WAR/FORCE/COMBAT   •   WAR AND REMEMBRANCE   •   WISDOM

WIT • WOMEN • WORDS • WORK PSYCHOLOGY • WRITING (INTEGRITY)

Walking

WALKING IS THE best possible exercise. Habituate yourself to walk very far.
—Thomas Jefferson

TAKE A TWO-MILE walk every morning before breakfast.   —Harry S Truman

WALK TILL THE blood appears on the cheek, but not the sweat on the brow.
—Spanish proverb

IF YOU CAN walk, don't drive. Think twice about using your car to go to work, to the drugstore, to a neighbor's house. Once you get in the walking habit, you'll hate using your automobile. . . . Walk barefoot. It's healthful for your feet and great for your legs. Best is going without shoes on grass or sand. —Sharon Gold

I'M AS BUSY as ever, and that's the secret when you get older. Don't stop working, always keep busy and keep active, that's important. . . . I always watch my weight. I'm always on a diet. And walk, always walk, that's the best way to keep in shape. I walk five to six miles a day.   —Louis J. Lefkowitz, at 77

THE SUM OF the whole is this: walk and be happy; walk and be healthy. The best way to lengthen our days is to walk steadily and with a purpose. The wandering man knows of certain ancients, far gone in years, who have staved off infirmities and dissolution by earnest walking—hale fellows, close up on ninety, but brisk as boys.   —Charles Dickens

War/Force/Combat

WHEN YOU APPEAL to force, there's one thing you must never do—lose.

—Dwight D. Eisenhower

WHEN YOU STRIKE at a king, you must kill him. —Ralph Waldo Emerson

> In peace, there's nothing so becomes a man
> As modest stillness, and humility;
> But when the blast of war blows in our ears,
> Then imitate the action of the tiger,
> Stiffen the sinews, summon up the blood . . .
> Now set the teeth and stretch the nostril wide,
> Hold hard the breath, and bend up every spirit
> to its full height!

—King Henry, in Shakespeare's
The Life of King Henry V

IN PLANNING ANY operation, it is vital to remember, and constantly repeat to oneself, two things: "In war nothing is impossible, provided you use audacity," and "Do not take counsel of your fears."

DON'T BE A fool and die for your country. Let the other sonofabitch die for his.

—George S. Patton

HIT HARD, HIT fast, hit often. —William Frederick ("Bull") Halsey

IF YOU WANT to win your battles, take an' work your bloomin' guns.

—Rudyard Kipling

WHEN FORCE IS necessary, there it must be applied boldly, decisively and completely. But one must know the limitations of force; one must know when to blend force with a maneuver, the blow with an agreement.   —Leon Trotsky

BEWARE LEST IN your anxiety to avoid war you obtain a master.—Demosthenes

LET HIM WHO does not know what war is go to war.   —Spanish proverb

THE WAY TO win an atomic war is to make certain it never starts.

—Omar N. Bradley

THE ART OF war is simple enough. Find out where your enemy is. Get at him as soon as you can. Strike him as hard as you can, and keep moving.

—Ulysses S. Grant

War and Remembrance

Take up our quarrel with the foe:
To you from failing hands we throw
The torch; be yours to hold it high.
If ye break faith with us who die
We shall not sleep, though poppies grow
   in Flanders fields.

—John McCrae

REMEMBER THE ALAMO!

REMEMBER THE MAINE!

REMEMBER PEARL HARBOR.   —War slogans

I HAVE FAITH that the human spirit will prove equal to the long heavy task of ending war. Against the pessimistic mood of our time, I think that the human spirit . . . is in essence heroic. . . . The beginning of the end of War lies in Remembrance.

—Herman Wouk, in the Foreword

to *War and Remembrance*

Wisdom

Be wise with speed
A fool at forty is a fool indeed.

—Edward Young

IF YOU WOULD thoroughly know anything, teach it to others. —Tryon Edwards

DO NOT BE fooled into believing that because a man is rich he is necessarily smart. There is ample proof to the contrary. —Julius Rosenwald

THE ART OF being wise is the art of knowing what to overlook.—William James

BETTER BE WISE by the misfortunes of others than by your own. —Aesop

Defer not till tomorrow to be wise,
Tomorrow's sun to thee may never rise.

—William Congreve

IT IS UNWISE to be too sure of one's own wisdom. It is healthy to be reminded that the strongest might weaken and the wisest might err. —Mohandas K. Gandhi

IN YOUTH ACQUIRE that which may requite you for the deprivations of old age; and if you are mindful that old age has wisdom for its food, you will so exert yourself in youth, that your old age will not lack sustenance.

—Leonardo da Vinci

MIX WITH YOUR sage counsels some brief folly. In due place to forget one's wisdom is sweet. —Cicero

CONSIDER THE LITTLE mouse, how sagacious an animal it is which never entrusts its life to one hole only. —Titus Maccius Plautus

Wit

IF YOU CAN'T be funny, be interesting. —Harold Ross, founder of *The New Yorker*

JUDGE NOT OF a jest when you have done laughing. —William Lloyd

He must not laugh at his own wheeze
A snuff box has no right to sneeze.

—Keith Preston

WIT OUGHT TO be a glorious treat, like caviar; never spread it about like marmalade. —Sir Noel Coward

Women

BOAST NOT THYSELF to know women, for thou knowest not what the next damsel shall teach thee. —Gelett Burgess

LOVE AND RESPECT woman. Look to her not only for comfort, but for strength and inspiration and the doubling of your intellectual and moral powers. Blot out from your mind any idea of superiority; you have none. —Joseph Mazzini

WHEREVER YOU GO, have a woman friend. —Irish proverb

NEVER TRY TO impress a woman, because if you do she'll expect you to keep up to the standard for the rest of your life. —W. C. Fields

ALWAYS BEGIN WITH a woman by telling her that you don't understand women. You will be able to prove it to her satisfaction more certainly than anything else you will ever tell her. —Don Marquis

THE NEXT YOUNG woman that comes to you—look at her with new eyes. Treat her first as a person, not as a young woman. For that, I think, is essentially what the new image of woman is: a person first, a woman second. Think about it and then change your image of women. —Arvonne S. Fraser

HONOR WOMEN! THEY entwine and weave heavenly roses in our earthly life. —Johann von Schiller

GIVE NOT THY soul unto a woman. —Ecclesiasticus

THINK FIRST YE women, to look to your behavior. The face pleases when character commends. Love of character is lasting; beauty will be ravaged by age. —Ovid

WATCH OUT FOR women's tricks! —From the Libretto of Mozart's *The Magic Flute*

IF WOMEN ARE expected to do the same work as men, we must teach them the same things. —Plato

WOMEN CLAIM THAT they want equal rights, equal respect, equal willingness to share domestic duties from their men. To win respect and the willingness to share domestic duties, women must be equally responsible for aspects of living together that are traditionally in the man's domain. Examples: balancing the checkbook, repairing broken furniture, mowing the lawn, finding the right stocks to invest in. You don't get respect because you want it; you get respect

because you earn it by being competent, intelligent, trustworthy, flexible, and generous.
—Marion A. Asnes

Words

SAY ALL YOU have to say in the fewest possible words, or your reader will be sure to skip them; and in the plainest possible words or he will certainly misunderstand them.
—John Ruskin

LET NO MAN deceive you with vain words.
—New Testament

BROADLY SPEAKING, THE short words are the best, and the old words best of all.
—Sir Winston Churchill

WHENEVER YOU CAN, shorten a sentence. And one always can. . . . Caress your sentence tenderly; it will end by smiling at you.
—Anatole France

WORDS MUST BE weighed, not counted.
—Polish proverb

AS TO THE adjective: when in doubt, strike it out.
—Mark Twain

ALWAYS SEEK THE hard, definite, personal word.
—T. E. Hulme

DO NOT ACCUSTOM yourself to use big words for little matters.—Samuel Johnson

WORDS HAVE WEIGHT, sound and appearance; it is only by considering these that you can write a sentence that is good to look at and good to listen to.
—W. Somerset Maugham

YOU CAN STROKE people with words.
—F. Scott Fitzgerald

LET US DEMAND that words be placed in a sentence where they logically belong, provided only that they do not defy idiom—and let us not imagine that idioms come into being overnight.

—Theodore M. Bernstein

GRASP THE SUBJECT, the words will follow.

—Cato the Elder

1. NEVER USE A long word where a short one will do.
2. If it is possible to cut out a word, always cut it out.
3. Never use the passive where you can use the active.
4. Never use a foreign phrase, a scientific word or a jargon word if you can think of an everyday English equivalent.
5. Break any of these rules sooner than say anything barbarous.

—George Orwell
"Politics and the English Language"

Work Psychology

NEVER SIT IN the place of a man who can say to you, "Rise."   —Arab proverb

DO PLEASANT THINGS yourself, but unpleasant things through others.

—Baltasar Gracian

NEVER LET YOUR inferiors do you a favor—it will be extremely costly.

—H. L. Mencken

NEVER BEFRIEND THE oppressed unless you are prepared to take on the oppressor.

—Ogden Nash

IF YOU SUSPECT a man, don't employ him, and if you employ him, don't suspect him.

—Chinese proverb

YOU HAVE SAT too long here for any good you have been doing. Depart, I say, and let us have done with you. In the name of God, go.   —Oliver Cromwell

NEVER MAKE A defense or an apology until you are accused.
                                        —Charles I, King of England

THERE ARE NEVER ten ways to do something. Only one. That is a question of morality. You have to be true to yourself and others.   —Jeanne Moreau

IF YOU SCATTER thorns, don't go barefoot.   —Italian proverb

NOTHING IS PARTICULARLY hard if you divide it into small jobs.—Henry Ford

"TRY TO HANDLE each piece of paper only once." Every time you pick up a piece of paper needing your action, failing to act only means you'll have to double your time and energy spent on it by picking it up again.—Michael LeBoeuf

WORK SMARTER, NOT harder.   —Ron Carswell

SERVA ME, SERVABO te. (Serve me and I will serve you.)   —Petronius

SCRATCH MY BACK and I'll scratch yours.   —American proverb

BETTER TO RELY on one powerful king than on many little princes.
                                        —Jean de La Fontaine

PUT NOT YOUR trust in princes.   —Georg Buchner

(*See also* Advertising, Business, Labor, and Management.)

Writing (Integrity)

Write 'till your ink be dry; and with your tears
Moist it again; and frame some feeling line,
That may discover such integrity.

—Proteus, in Shakespeare's
Two Gentlemen of Verona

ONE MAY WRITE from the outside of his mind, as it were; write and write, learnedly and eloquently, and make no impression; but when he speaks from real insight and conviction of his own, men are always glad to hear him, whether they agree with him or not. Get down to your real self . . . and let that speak. One's real self is always vital, and gives the impression of vitality.

—John Burroughs

NEVER ALLOW THE integrity of your own way of seeing things and saying things to be swamped by the influence of a master, however great.

—George P. Lathrop

WRITE SOMETHING TO suit yourself and many people will like it; write something to suit everybody and scarcely anyone will care for it.   —Jesse Stuart

KEEP YOUR HANDS from literary picking and stealing. But if you cannot refrain from this kind of stealth, abstain from murdering what you steal.

—Augustus Toplady

NEVER PURSUE LITERATURE as a trade. —Samuel Taylor Coleridge

(*See also* Literary Composition.)

Youth

PRAISE YOUTH AND it will prosper. —Irish proverb

DON'T LAUGH AT a youth for his affectations; he is only trying on one face after another to find his own. —Logan Pearsall Smith

DON'T LET YOURSELF forget what it's like to be sixteen. —Anonymous

KEEP TRUE TO the dreams of thy youth. —Johann von Schiller

BE GENTLE WITH the young. —Juvenal

Index

Index

Index

ABOUT THE AUTHORS

WILLIAM SAFIRE is the Pulitzer-Prize-winning political and language columnist for *The New York Times*, and author of *What's the Good Word?*, among other books. He added an "e" to the family name because that is how the name is pronounced. His brother, LEONARD SAFIR, a former television executive, is the editor of *Perspective*—three management newsletters produced for Norton Simon, Inc.